Guarded by Faith

by the same author
Time for Unity (S.C.M. Press)

Guarded by Faith

Oliver Tomkins
Bishop of Bristol

HODDER AND STOUGHTON
LONDON SYDNEY AUCKLAND TORONTO

To all my friends in Bristol
out of whose patience this book was born

Acknowledgments

I am conscious of indebtedness to many, most of whom I trust are acknowledged in the text itself.

I would particularly like to thank Dr. Dillistone for allowing me to draw so much upon his thought in his *Christian Understanding of Atonement* which I happened to read whilst preparing these lectures; and to Dr. Appleton, Archbishop in Jerusalem, whose little book, *One Man's Prayers*, contains many treasures besides the two I quote.

I am grateful to Messrs. Blackwell for permission to quote in Chapter Three the comparatively unknown and early poem by the late Dorothy Sayers.

Where indicated, biblical quotations are from the New English Bible, New Testament, second edition, © 1970 by permission of Oxford and Cambridge Universities.

I would also express my gratitude to Mrs. Dorothy Amesbury and Miss Peggy Blair-Brown for their patience in typing and re-typing successive drafts, and to the latter for preparing the index.

Bristol: July 1970

Contents

Introduction

This book had its origin in a series of talks I gave during Lent 1969 as part of a 'Year of Renewal' in the Diocese of Bristol, a renovation for us all at the end of ten years of my being a bishop.

The audience aimed at was—and is—the kind of church-goer who asks serious questions about the way Christianity comes over in its traditional forms and the kind of person on the fringe of the Church who wonders whether the Church has anything credible to say at all. There are some church-goers who are not asking the questions I here try to answer. There are many non-church-goers who would want to start much further back. This is not for either group. And I am very conscious that for many people, the questions they ask are not to be answered in *words* at all. The trouble is that it is Christian living which is unconvincing. As James Baldwin, the American Negro writer, said to the Uppsala Assembly—"I shall no longer listen to what you say, but I shall watch very carefully what you do." No little book will do much to deal with that situation.

I am conscious, too, of the limited value of 'apologetics' in commending Christianity at any time. As Coleridge once wrote: "I more than fear the prevailing taste for books of Natural Theology, Physico-theology, Demonstrations of God from Nature, Evidences of Christianity and the like. *Evidences of Christianity*—I am weary of the word. Make a man *feel* his *want* of it: rouse him if you can to the self-knowledge of his *need* for it; and you can safely trust to its own evidence—remembering only this, the express declaration of Christ himself: 'No man cometh to me unless the Father leadeth him.'"[1] I have tried always to start from real interests and felt needs, the things which are important to us as human beings, Christian or not, old or young—and then go on to try to draw out what I believe that the Bible and the Christian tradition have to offer to what we really care about.

Here is an attempt to combine the traditional role of a bishop as a 'guardian of the Faith' with an invitation to genuine open discussion.

This raises a double difficulty:

    (a) Can you combine these two?
    (b) Can you separate them?

(a) How can a genuine discussion be combined with the Christian claim to 'finality'. Christianity claims to be not just a 'point of view'—but the Truth. Some hate this claim: others love it. So this lays one open to suspicion from both parties.

Enquirers are always sceptical about Christian honesty and disinterestedness. They suspect that we are tied by the leg—bound to reach certain conclusions; a B.B.C. friend of mine was working on a programme about religious experience which involved co-operating with an agnostic scientist—who said, after hours of discussion; "But you aren't interested in arriving at the *truth* are you?" Some are likely to be doubly suspicious of a bishop, thinking it is more than his job is worth not to arrive at

[1] *Aids to Reflection*, new edition, p. 272.

official conclusions. Part of the interest in *Honest to God* was in seeing a bishop asking real questions and not necessarily finding the respectable answers.

Christians who value the 'tradition' have always suspected the 'explorers'. It is instructive to look back over Christian history—even recent English Church history—to see how new ideas in scholarship have always been howled down.[2] Church leaders have a duty to resist error, but it may not be at the price of muzzling scholarship.

(b) Can expounding the faith be *separated* from enquiry and speculation? Recent Roman Catholic writers on Vatican II have distinguished between *depositum fidei* and *modus explicandi*. In theory, it is an admirable distinction—but it soon leads to trouble when it appears that in modifying the 'way of putting it' you are altering 'the faith once delivered'. We are bound to run this risk if it seems that the *modus* of a previous age now actually obscures the faith—at least for some people. It is a risk we have to take because different people are at different stages in their appreciation of religious language. I was preaching at Michaelmas last year to a congregation containing many young people from school juniors to late teenagers. Knowing from other young people that the conventional picture of angels—as sexless human beings with wings—was as unreal as fairies, I said that this picture-language must not be taken literally if it would blind us to the New Testament conviction that God actively protects and communicates with mankind. I got an indignant

[2] E.g. Roger Lloyd, *The Church of England, 1900–1965* (S.C.M. Press, 1966), p. 115.

letter from an older person for 'de-bunking angels' which she had been teaching children to believe in.

We live in an age when the forms and images of Christendom have lost their vitality for millions of our contemporaries. Christians may yet become fewer still —and the burdens we carry become heavier—whether it be the shrines which our forbears built or the language and rites which once vibrated with life. Meanwhile, we struggle to discover which parts of our heritage can be revitalised and which we leave behind as dead. But the living God goes forward still and calls us to follow along a narrow path which it is often hard to discern.

In such an exploratory situation, it is doubtful whether a bishop can be a 'leader' at all. A bishop is, by definition, a *representative* man, called to care equally for the student to whom a violent demonstration is the highest form of honesty and the lifelong church-goer who will not receive the body and blood of Christ on the Sundays when the vicar uses the 'new Communion service'.

In the spate of religious books, I only dare to offer this one because some people have already found help from watching this particular bishop trying to walk on a tight-rope instead of sitting on the fence. It is not we who are 'guardians of the faith'. It is faith which guards us.

The Living God

Let all the world in ev'ry corner sing,
My God and King.

George Herbert, *The Temple*

The more I thought about undertaking public addresses
on religion the more foolish and inadequate did it seem
to me to offer to stand up and just talk about God or to
sit down and write about him. If I want to convey to
you anything of what I really feel about God, and if
we are to join together in anything that is at all adequate,
we ought to shout and sing and dance, we ought to join
together in declaiming great poetry or pouring out the
loveliest music ever dreamed of. Just to deal in words
seems so inadequate. Or we ought not to be doing that
at all, but be out somewhere where we are needed, by a
sickbed or rescuing junkies from their rat-infested
cellars or feeding the hungry or almost anything but
just dealing in words. But having written that much as
I set out in this task, I realised that the first kind of
thing does, in fact, happen after a fashion Sunday by
Sunday and all the year round in our churches, because
a Choral Eucharist is a sort of domesticated version of
the ecstasy which made King David dance before the
Ark, to the great embarrassment of his wife.[1] And our
church choirs do try to capture an echo of the heavenly
music which Bach and Mozart may be imagined as
writing still for the Almighty. And so perhaps I might

[1] I Chronicles 5:29.

as well go on, although my words will fall as far short
of the divine wisdom as church services fall short of
the heavenly ecstasy. As to the sick and the junkies and
the starving, they are all outside our walls still and they
will be there all right tomorrow and next week. And
Jesus will be out there with them too as he always is
and was and will be. These words may be justified if they
make us a little more sensitive to the voice which said,
"Inasmuch as ye did it unto one of the least of these my
brethren ye did it unto me".

I have never found belief in God easy. Although I was
brought up in a Christian home, I have had to struggle
to find such faith as I have and belief for me has always
had to walk the knife-edge where disbelief lies on each
side. But faith has come partly through other people
directly, through lives I admired whose own motive
power was their faith, and it has come partly through
other people *indirectly,* through ideas in books. So I
know that faith can be strengthened both by personal
contact and through ideas conveyed by words. So, on
that understanding, let us search for the right words.

*   *   *

Words can be maddening things. We cannot ever say
all we mean or feel, and yet we cannot do without words.
In particular, religious language can both convey religious truth and impede or confuse it. I do not for one
moment forget that much religious truth is conveyed not
by words but by actions. But for the moment we are
concerned with words, so let us begin to consider what
it means to talk about God at all, remembering always that if there is a God to talk about we can never
do so without at the same time talking to him.

In talking about God, we are talking about something quite different from anything else we ever talk about. If this were not so it would not be about *God* that we were talking. God, if the word means anything at all, is bound to be beyond description, beyond comprehension, beyond analysis. All great religions agree on this. To say anything about God on the assumption that you can say it in a way that is exactly comparable with what we can say about anything else is to cease to talk about God. Even to say *God is* is misleading, if we suppose that God exists in the same sense that anything else exists. As Paul Tillich puts it in one of his books, "God does not exist. He is being—itself, beyond essence and existence."[2] Therefore to argue that God exists is to deny him, which just shows you the limitations of words in trying to describe what I am trying to describe. So should I now stop and just ask you to contemplate, but to contemplate what?

All religions worthy of the name agree that nothing we can say about God is adequate; but they would not be religions at all if they did not go on to say that the search for the least inadequate ways of talking about him is the highest calling of the human mind. We can never say anything about God which is not in itself misleading. But we can never cease to try to say things which, as far as they go, are true.

So, before we go any further, it may be worth asking—what language about God is like. All talk about God is bound to be picture-language, i.e. language drawn from the familiar experiences to describe *aspects* of what, in its fullness, is beyond experience. For example, all language about Heaven (whatever that means) is in 'pictures' of light, jewels, worship and so forth, because it is, by definition, something beyond the normal:

[2] *Systematic Theology* (Nisbet, 1953–1957), v. 1. p. 227.

but remember that romantic love is described by the poets largely in picture-language too—because love also is something which transcends the commonplace.

I would distinguish, to help us to know how we are talking when we talk of God both now and in later chapters, between three pairs of characteristics of religious language which have to be kept in balance within themselves.

(i) *Religious language involves both faith and reason.* For example, when the New Testament describes St. Peter as saying "Thou art the Christ" or St. Thomas crying out "My Lord and My God," each was making an act of faith. Each was expressing complete trust and yet each had a background of reason for what he said: St. Peter his understanding of what his Jewish tradition meant by the word 'Christ', the Messiah; St. Thomas that he accepted the evident reality of Christ's risen presence. So the language of faith is never credulity but it always goes beyond mere analysis.

(ii) *Religious language always involves both commitment and detachment.* Religious language is always highly personal; 'This is true for me.' This emphasis upon true *for me* is part of the meaning of the now fashionable word 'existentialism'. And yet the word 'true' is meaningless unless it can contain the possibility that it is true for you too. That is to say that it was true before I saw it, objectively true in a sense detachable from my ability to see that it is true.

(iii) *Religious language is always both symbolic and descriptive.* To speak of God as king, or even as father, is to use symbols, pictures, and yet that can have no meaning unless it is in part to describe something with which we are already familiar. Some of the 'Death of God' talk is due to losing this particular balance, that is to confuse the symbol with the description, so that if you can no longer describe God as a white-haired old monarch sitting on a throne in the sky, if that as a symbol is dead, it need not follow that the reality it symbolised is dead as well.

"The 'Death of God' syndrome can only occur where the controlling symbols of the culture have been more or less uncritically fused with the transcendent God."[3]

At this point, we might pause to reflect upon the impossibility and yet the necessity of what we are attempting to do, to use words to describe the indescribable; the attempt to get our minds round that being which, if we fully understood it, would thereby have ceased to be God. Consider a few sentences from one of those writers who saw this most clearly. It was Saint Augustine who, walking one day on the seashore, saw a child with a bucket trying to empty the sea into a hole which he had dug. And Augustine realised that this was a picture of the human mind trying to take in God. Then at the beginning of his *Confessions* (i.4) he writes this, "What art thou then my God? What but the Lord God? for who is Lord but the Lord, or who is God save our God? And yet what have I now said—my God, my life, my holy joy? Or what can any man say when he speaks of Thee? yet woe to him who does not speak, since dumb are even the most eloquent".

Reflect for a moment on the significance of such a struggle to say the unsayable. Why have so many minds for so long felt that they must attempt this impossibility?

All religions worthy of the name think of God as the most real reality. But is God for you the most real thing there is? Some perhaps would honestly answer 'yes'.

[3] See H. Cox, *On Not Leaving it to the Snake* (S.C.M. Press, 1968), p. 5.

Others would say frankly 'no' and others might hesitate because you wonder what is most real for you. And having located it, you wonder whether it may in some way be related to God.

There are two areas of our experience which I believe everybody would unhesitatingly call real. *The world*, as we know it around us, and secondly and especially *other people*. So let us look more closely at what we mean by calling those real.

So far as *the world* as a whole is concerned, different aspects of it are more real to some than to others. But for many people it is the world described by science, the world you can measure. We know a lot more about that world than our forefathers did. We know that it took a very long time to reach its present stage, so that (to use one picture which I can always remember), if you can imagine a film showing the history of the entire world from its beginnings which lasted for twenty-four hours, only the last five seconds of it would show human life. We know that our planet is one of nine circling round a sun which is itself perhaps one of thirty thousand million suns in this galaxy and that this galaxy is perhaps ten million million million miles away from the next nearest one. We know that atomic exploration has changed our ideas about solid matter and that the world is basically energy and that new forms and uses of energy are being discovered almost every day. It is being aware of such facts as these that makes modern men and women modern, for it is in this that we differ from generations before us. We expect continued discovery; we expect the extension of man's control over nature to go on. We shall enlarge our understanding of space, of the microscopic atom, of the control of disease, so that more and more of life will come under human

control. It is true that man's control of *himself* lags
behind, but in principle there is good reason to believe
that that can be enlarged too. Education, psychology,
genetics, state-planning and the rest, all give confidence
to modern man that, given time, we could manage ourselves as well. It is this confidence that distinguishes
modern man from our predecessors. Earlier ages felt
that vast areas of life could only be accepted, not controlled; disease, famine, the weather, were just things
you had to take. This is what lies behind the much-used
phrase about 'man come of age'. We are prepared to
take responsibility for our world. This has narrowed
considerably the area in which people used to call in
God. It still survives in insurance policies as 'acts of
God'. But a 'God of the gaps' has less and less manoeuv-
ring space. It is true that death remains, at best only
postponed. But that too can be accepted as part of evolution and the price of the emergence of the new.

How does all this affect the Christian picture of the
Creator? Certainly we cannot think of a God who made
it all and then left it to run itself, except for intervening
every now and again in the way of miracles. That is a
caricature of what Christians have ever believed, though
there are some people who, thinking that that is the
Christian view, have rejected it. But to try to see how
God is related to the marvels of nature has always been
a Christian concern. A great predecessor of mine gave
his life to thinking about it in his day, and there is a
splendid epitaph in Bristol Cathedral (attributed to his
admirer, Robert Southey) on Joseph Butler, Bishop of
Bristol from 1738 to 1750 and author of *The Analogy of
Religion.* "It was reserved for him to develop the
Analogy of Christianity to the constitution and course

of Nature, and laying his strong foundations in the depth of that great argument, there to construct another and irrefragable proof, thus rendering Philosophy subservient to Faith." I think that somewhat overestimates the achievement of Bishop Butler, but my point is he did *try*.

The Bible is rich with insights into how to think of creation. First of all in the Genesis story, which is not of course history but illustrates how God was 'in the beginning' to bring about the world we know, with man as a continuous part with all that is and yet distinguished from it by being given authority and stewardship in it. And the Old Testament continues the story by seeing God's strategy as the special calling of some people for the sake of all. Thus, history is a meaningful process all through. We shall think in the next chapter how the Messiah, the Christ, is central to that strategy, but the immediate point is that the Bible sees world history as having a personal meaning. It is not a blind succession, but it has a will running through it. God is not only the beginning and right through, but also the end of the process. The New Testament is full of picture-language, inevitably since alluding to something not yet experienced, about how God will finally make sense of the whole story in his judgment and mercy.

All this already lies in embryo, as it were, in the biblical picture, and the history of Christian reflection about it is the story of how these insights develop as men unpack more and more of the meaning of creation. In Christian thinking today there are two rather different streams of interpretation, seeking to do justice on the one hand to 'man come of age', man obeying his call to stewardship and responsibility, taking more and more responsibility for the world, and on the other hand 'man in evolution', part of a grand cosmic design. The one stream is represented by thinkers like Bonhoeffer and the other stream by thinkers like Teilhard de Chardin (the Roman Catholic priest who was also a palaeontologist and anthropologist). But the point I want to stress here is that in order to speak of God at all to our modern world, we need to draw upon biblical insights into God as Creator which do justice *both* (a) to the way he has given to man *responsibility for the world,* which entitles and indeed obliges him to explore it and to shoulder the consequences, and (b) to see man *as part of the world*, part of God's own design, a majestic, big-scale plan for bringing man as the crown of creation into ever more sensitive and complex relationship to nature and to humanity. The Christian doctrine of God as Creator is being seen in our time as a more exciting, dynamic, purposeful interpretation of the kind of world we live in than ever it was before. If our experience of the world is one of the things most real to us, as to me it is, then I must say that I also find that the attempt to interpret it in terms of a Creator God who is big enough to be the beginning, the middle and the end of it all, a God big enough to take responsibility for the whole amazing, confusing, ugly and splendid business, this is a more exciting and more real thing to be attempted than I ever dreamed it could be.

I have chosen to start from the world as known by science because for many people today that is the most real and exciting.

But there are some for whom the most *real* is not science but *the arts*—music, painting, poetry, drama. It is in these that you come to that mysterious edge of things—the point at which you glimpse, or take off into, infinity.

For such, there needs to be a transposition into another key of what I have been saying about the Creator—seeing him less in terms of an artificer and more in terms of a supreme *artist or composer*. That aspect we shall return to when we consider the meaning of worship.

The second aspect of experience which seems to all of us to be 'real' is the fact of *other people*. The Christian creed says, "I believe in God, the *Father*, Maker of Heaven and Earth". All that I have said so far could be rather impersonal, describable in such terms as the Ultimate Cause and End, the Ground of our Being and such like. It is our experience of other people which begins to throw light upon why the Creator may be called *Father*.

The essence of our experience of other people is that in them we discover other independent sources of being. We become aware of ourselves by being aware of others as also beings who, like ourselves, have a will, a centre of experience, a demand upon us to which we must respond by respecting it as we wish to be respected. We can ignore that in others—and try to push them around, to ignore them, to use and manipulate them—but only at the cost of knowing that we are violating in them something which we do not wish them to violate in ourselves. We all hate to be treated as 'things', simply to be ignored or used. Why?

This was all worked out in a little book by a Jew, Martin Buber, *I and Thou*—one of the seminal books in my lifetime. Like all great books—it seems so obvious once someone has said it. Buber distinguished between *I—it* and *I—thou* relationship; *I—it* is all that area in

which we approach all that outside ourselves which we
can use and manipulate without responding; *I—thou*
is all the area in which we are conscious of meeting
another 'I' who addresses us as 'thou'. That is the starting point (there are many ramifications) but the heart
of this thesis is that what we mean by God is that being
who is always the 'I' who addresses us as 'thou' and
whom we can never address as 'it'. He is the centre from
whom all other 'centres' derive the awareness of themselves. Buber was a Jew, and he was re-affirming an
essential biblical insight: that God, if he is God at all, is
always the living God; the God who calls people, who
makes them realise who they are by addressing them
and evoking a response; the God of Abraham and of
Isaac and of Jacob; the God who takes the initiative and
seeks men. Just as in our dealings with each other we
only become fully alive as we respond to personal relationships, so the final meaning of our existence is
revealed as we become aware that the heart of reality is
personal, a Someone not just a something, who gives us
our significance by calling one of us by name. This much
the Jews of the Old Testament had seen. Jesus, as a
Jew, took that insight and lifted it to a new level of
intimacy and lived it out in a unique completeness of
trust. That is why he said, 'when you pray say Abba,
Father'. Abba is the Aramaic word of his time for
Daddy, Papa—the childlike word of absolute intimacy
and absolute dependence. To speak of God as a Christian
is to dare to accept all that is most real to us in our experience of encountering other people as real people,
another 'I' who addresses us as 'thou'—and to see that
this is a valid insight into our relation to reality, that
the same being who is the Creator of all this complex

universe is one to whom we can respond with the personal trust of a child to a father. But, to see more fully how we dare do so takes us on to the next theme—what it means to see Jesus as 'God with us', the God-Man.

The God-Man

For Man is ev'ry thing, and more:
He is a tree, yet bears no fruit ...
Since then, my God, thou hast
So brave a Palace built; O dwell in it.

George Herbert, *The Temple*

"To be human is to be concerned with persons." Christians and humanists would alike agree. To be human is to care about other humans. This lies at the heart of all the generous causes which move men and women today. The peace movement is basically a hatred of war because of what it does to people. The enthusiasm and self-sacrifice which go into Oxfam, War on Want, Shelter and Christian Aid; the kind of concern which lies behind 'human rights' or 'conservation'; all comes down simply to a concern for people. International organisation or legislation for social justice are in the end of the day also justified by their concern for people, for people in general. There can only be *effectual* concern for people in general if it is turned into legislation or organisation. Justice is love generalised. (Herein lies the inevitability of a Christian concern for politics). But when we begin to ask 'Why do people matter?'—we then face one of those questions to which there is no answer outside itself. You can only say 'Because they do'. People matter because people matter. It is an act of faith, sometimes called 'a self-authenticating experience'; something you do not need to argue about, it is just there.

But although the question does not need anything outside itself to furnish the answer, the answer itself raises further questions. This is illustrated in a book by a Professor of Social Studies [1] dealing with the work of psychiatrists, psychiatric social workers, child-care officers, the medical profession and all those whose job it is to give counsel to people. There is much emphasis nowadays on 'non-directive counselling', that is to say that the job of a good counsellor is not to impose his own point of view on other people or to take their decisions for them, but to assist them to uncover their own dilemmas and make their own decisions. But Professor Halmos points out that all those who are counsellors do, in fact, have certain assumptions of faith, which make sense of their jobs: the faith, though it is not demonstrable in any logical way, that love is better than hatred, that harmony is better than disharmony, that co-operation is better than conflict and so forth. In other words, 'non-directive' can be all right as a description of a method but it is futile to imagine that it can be raised into a philosophy. Translated into theological terms, the question might be phrased 'Do people matter because they matter to God?' or if that sounds too pious 'Do people and the universe somehow fit together?' If so, people matter because their significance is in some way part of the significance of all that is.

The Christian religion begins in a man, Jesus, who came to have for his followers a significance that they could only express by saying that to them he had the *value* of God. The first four centuries of Christian thinking were very much occupied with trying to hammer out

[1] See Paul Halmos, *The Faith of the Counsellors* (Constable, 1965).

how you can express the belief that Jesus is in some real way both man and God.[2]

Let us start from the simplest New Testament confession of faith, *Jesus is Christ and Lord*. There are three names or titles here which need to be examined in turn.

(i) *Jesus*: an historical, personal name. Was there really a knowable historical figure? That used to be a fairly simple question to answer, when most people were able to think of the Bible as literal history right through, reliable in all its details. But it is impossible nowadays to think in quite so simple way about the Bible. It is now common knowledge, (though of course theological students have been aware of it from very early centuries) that what we commonly talk about as 'a book', the Bible, is in fact a library. It contains many different kinds of books, history, legend, poetry, devotion, hymns—all sorts of writing bound up in that one book, books of different dates, different purposes, different character. One of the words which has been bandied about in a good deal of recent discussion to describe some elements in the Bible is the word *myth*. It is an unfortunate word because, although it is a perfectly proper theological term in its place, for ordinary people the word 'myth' is more or less synonymous with 'fairly tale.' People think that if you call a thing a myth you are really putting it in exactly the same category as the old pagan stories as, for example, about the way in which the gods became men or turned girls into laurel bushes. That is not its theological meaning. It means a way of speaking of truths which are more than local, historical facts. In using picture language to describe something more than mere facts, interpretation is combined with description.

[2] For a serious and lively consideration of this theme, see *The Glory of Man* by David Jenkins (S.C.M. Press, 1962).

An illuminating comparison is to think of the difference between a photograph and a painting. Some paintings are very close to photographs. They are scrupulous in their exact representation of what is to be seen and, to all intents and purposes, you might as well have taken a photograph as have done the painting. At the other extreme, some paintings are so far from representation that it is hard to guess their meaning unless you have had clues to a particular way of thinking which lies behind the artist's mind, like the fascinating painting by Salvador Dali, in which a large watch lies limply over a rock like a piece of melting butter. That kind of painting can only be understood if you share an understanding of psychoanalysis and its interpretation which he is trying to portray. So, when on radio or T.V., theologians speak about the early chapters of Genesis as *myth*, the story of the Creation and the Fall of Adam, they are far from saying that this is a fairy tale which you can dismiss. It is not being belittled but dignified by being called a myth, in that this is a vivid pictorial way of both interpreting and describing the origins and the status of man.

So, too, the word myth is used of elements in the gospels, since they also are to be thought of not so much as photographs but as paintings. Take an analogy from that lovely tradition of painting, especially developed in the Eastern Orthodox Church in Russia, of icons. Although an icon invariably portrays human beings or beasts in ways that are recognisably human beings or horses or goats, yet there is something about the way in which an icon is arranged, something about the proportions and the flow of the lines, the subtle juxtaposition or emotional suggestion of the colours, and the pattern which they all make which removes it far from photography and makes it essentially a work of interpretation.

This, I suggest, is the right way to think about the gospels. Every Evangelist was, in his own way, an artist as well as an historian, combining description and interpretation. When you look at the Passion story in the four gospels you notice the distinct differences of angle or interpretation; so that you may say that in St. Matthew the cross of Christ is seen as the fulfilment of the Old Testament; in St. Mark it is portrayed as a scaffold where a real death takes place; in St. Luke it is a pulpit from which love and forgiveness are preached; in St. John it is a throne where Christ reigns in glory. But in spite of these differences of interpretation in the gospels, the impressive thing is the consistency of the person of Jesus which emerges, from many centuries of searching analysis and ruthless dissection of the documents. We do not need to be alarmed by swings of fashion in theology, though I think it is not just English pride which suggests that Continental Protestants have often shown more exaggerated swings, for the relation between English and German theology is the relation between the back and front wheels of a bicycle; the back wheel gets to the same place very soon after, but without wobbling about as much.

There are, and have been for a very long time, varieties of emphasis in New Testament interpretation. I would mention one or two in living memory. It is often not realised that Doctor Schweitzer, who died as a missionary legend, was in his early years far more notorious than John Robinson as a theologian! He produced a book, which appeared in England in 1910 under the title *The Quest of the Historical Jesus* which certainly fluttered the theological dovecotes by picturing Jesus as being deluded by his expectation of the imminent end of the world. Not long after that there came a very dif-

ferent swing of the pendulum by a distinguished son of
Bristol Grammar School, T. R. Glover, whose book *The
Jesus of History* presented Jesus as a good, early
twentieth-century liberal reformer. In our own time the
American writer, Dr. Altizer, one of the chief exponents
of the 'death of God' theology, has written to suggest
that in Jesus, God poured himself out without remain-
der, as it were, and in dying upon the cross, God died
too. This is the revival of a very ancient heresy ('Patri-
passionism'—the suffering of the Father) which blurred
the distinction between the Father and the Son so that
Altizer's theology has been summed up, "There is no
God and Jesus Christ is His Son". Yet another Jesus
bursts through in Dennis Potter's T.V. play, *The Son
of Man*, a tortured yet committed teacher, whose "Love
your enemies" is mocked by the dereliction in which he
is left to die. Down the ages the figure of Jesus fascinates
and tantalises—and always he breaks out of every
attempt to label and classify him. But, elusive though he
is, there is certainly somebody there. Ordinary Christians may go on reading the gospels with confidence as
interpretative portraits of a man who could never have
been simply invented. His character comes through too
sharply for that. He stands out clearly as one for whom
God as Father was intensely real, as one who saw life as
loving obedience to his Father, as one for whom service
of others was central, as one who was compassionate
and amazingly free in his personal dealings; as one who
exhibited power. Any given miracle described in the
gospels may be uncertain in its details and conflicting
accounts of it be given, but there can be no doubt that
around Jesus strange things happened. That is not the
end of what men came to see in him but it is the
beginning.

We need have no doubt at all that a man lived and a man died. He was a fact in history. The only unique clause in the creed is *under Pontius Pilate*. Other religions talk of a Creator God, and even call him Father, there are many religious legends of virgin births, of dying and rising Gods, Isis and Osiris and the rest. But Christianity stands or falls by Jesus as a fact of history and all attempts to disprove the fact have failed.

(ii) the second title which Jesus bears is *the Christ*. Jesus was not only a person in history. The turning point in the gospels is Peter's confession *Thou art the Christ*, the Messiah, the Anointed One whom the Jews expected to bring them God's kingdom.[3] God's kingdom is central in the teaching of Jesus. He picks up the hope of the Old Testament that God would somehow be vindicated. There is so much in the world to deny him. His own chosen people are conquered, enslaved, exiled; the wicked flourish, the good suffer. Something deep down in their faith cried out 'It can't go on, it's all wrong' and the Messiah is to be the one who should prove that God is right.

From one point of view the life of Jesus is the achievement of making clear what God's kingdom is like. He had to turn many ideas upside down in the process. He had to show that majesty means service—as in the lovely story in St. John about the foot-washing. He had to show that motives justify ritual and not the other way up; that the love of God does not coerce but suffers. It is an essential part of the interview with Peter that immediately after that confession of faith, Jesus affirms that the Son of Man *must* suffer. Only by dying could he

[3] See Mark 8:27-31.

unanswerably demonstrate what the kingdom of God is really like. The death of Jesus is integral to bringing in the kingdom.

At this point, let us isolate two aspects of the significance of the death of Jesus. The first is that *God accepts* us. God accepts us in spite of being the people we are. The sense of guilt takes many forms. Personal guilt has long been prominent in Christian piety and is deep in many of our hymns and in the whole tradition of Christian experience. But often today it is known or recognised more clearly in the form of isolation, in the sense of being rejected, of not belonging and so of being meaningless.[4] It is part of the meaning of redemption by the death of Christ to see it as the readiness of God to go on having dealings with us after we have done everything we can to reject him. This is a common experience of human living, e.g. the mother or the wife who fully receives back the returned prisoner. It is not an easy or cheap thing to do and the cross demonstrates the price that has to be paid for letting the whole weight of human resistance to love and rejection of it fall upon the person who most completely embodied love. To be able to believe this, to be able to hear God say, "It's all right, my dear, I accept you" is to be able to accept yourself and other people, to become a reconciled reconciler.

And secondly *Jesus on the Cross did something we cannot do for ourselves*. It is this realisation that underlies a number of traditional phrases like ransomed, bought at a price, Christ's death making satisfaction, being a substitution, a sacrifice for sin. All these ideas drawn from various ages and in varying language, are scattered throughout the Bible, the liturgy and our hymns and they are difficult and puzzling to many. That

[4] See more fully in Chapter 3.

is why the next chapter is concerned with going deeper into this aspect. But what they all have in common is that the man we see on the cross was really one of us, a man being all through his life what we recognise a man *ought* to be—and yet he hangs there dead. If living as you should live, leads to that—well, what is the point? The point is the Resurrection: that God accepted that life, that death, and gave it his seal of approval by raising Jesus from the dead. Jesus identified himself with mankind as we ought to be—and God identified himself with Jesus by showing that this is what He, the Father, is like.

(iii) The title 'Jesus is Lord' brings to a focus the faith in his resurrection and exaltation. It adds something more universal to Jesus as Christ and is in itself an example of Christianity raiding contemporary thought for new words. The 'Christ' was a Jewish idea, and in that context full of meaning, as we have seen. But the scattered Jews who first heard the gospel lived in a pagan world which was seeking for a 'Lord', one to whom worship and final loyalty could be given. One reason why I believe we shall some day see (or if not us, our children's children) a mighty renewal of Christian faith is because our world is so like the pagan world of the first centuries. Now, as then, there is a widespread desire for something—someone—worth trusting, giving value and significance to the whole of human experience.

To call Jesus 'Lord' has three implications worth exploring:

(a) It implies deliverance for Christians from fear of the *secular* and a re-personalising of the secular world. These words need explaining. First of all let us distinguish 'secular' as an adjective and 'secularise' as a verb from *secularism* which is a philosophy. That lively book by an American writer Harvey Cox, *The Secular City*, distinguishes between them by first of all defending 'secular' as a thoroughly biblical and Christian word. The biblical understanding of God's activity and victory in the world is in the proper sense a secular activity and victory, that is to say it is concerned with the realities of *history*; 'saeculum' means 'this age'. The biblical doctrine of creation freed man from thinking of the natural world as enchanted, full of friendly or fiendish demons. Instead the created order has a right to be itself. In the Old Testament books of the law, politics and economics are seen as a direct consequence of God's ordering of the world and not as they were, for example in the Egypt from which the Israelites were delivered, a by-product of the sacral kingship. Christianity, when it is true to its biblical origins, rejoices in 'the autonomy of the secular', a recognition that human society is pluriform. The many different departments of life have their own legitimacy and integrity, for the believing Christian, because they are part of the order which God himself has created and do not owe their legitimacy to any secondary source. In all areas of life there is a possibility that the honest pursuit of disciplines proper to that territory will lead to conformity with the will of the Creator. 'Secular*ism*' on the other hand is the false interpretation of this pluriform reality by presenting it as an end in itself. It is the explicit denial that the different aspects of human activity derive their independent dignity from the will of the Creator.

I first began to see this in the 1930s when I was assisting Dr. J. H. Oldham in the foundation of what came to be called the Christian Frontier Movement. He introduced me to the book by Jacques Maritain *True Humanism*. We were then on the verge of war and in this conception of 'true humanism' one discerned the outlines of a 'New Christendom' which would not be dominated by the Church attempting to rule all life or by theology attempting to rule all knowledge but a true 'harmonising of the autonomies', a glad recognition that all human activity carried out with integrity has a proper place in human existence, even when it is not consciously related to Christian faith. This implies a doctrine of creation which sees the logos (i.e. the meaning) inherent in things which only work properly if they work in God's way. This is a working out of the doctrine, implicit in the prologue to the fourth gospel[5] where the word, or the logos, of God is seen as the light which lightens every man coming into the world, the logos of God by which all things were made and without whom was not anything made that has been made. "He was in the world and the world was made by Him though the world knew Him not."

God is with us, among us, in the decisions and relationships of the secular city. He is there hidden and unknown, but we can trust his purpose even when we cannot yet name him. This is a true biblical and prophetic insight if really based in a living apprenhension of God. But the danger inherent in this approach is that it leads one to say that whatever is, is therefore right. How are we to distinguish the good from the bad in the way the world developes?

Things are not good just because they happen. There were those who commended Hitler's Germany because it began by curing unemployment and Mussolini's Italy

[5] See St. John 1 : 1–14.

because he succeeded in making the trains run punctually.[6]

One clue surely lies in whether this or that aspect of modern technological advance or political change can be vindicated because it leads to the deeper care for personality which a faith in Jesus Christ discerns as the meaning of human life. This is to bring us again to that criterion from which we began, that to be truly human is to care about persons. We must also be on our guard here lest our interpretation of what we mean by a person is unbiblical and unchristian in its individualism. Personality is only fully developed in community so that the Christian clue is personality-in-community and not mere individualism.

(b) This recognition of Jesus as Lord also implies a new basis for proclaiming judgment and mercy. If our discernment of the immanence of God in a true secular development is to be fully Christian it involves the recognition of the transcendence of God in judgment. This means that to proclaim Jesus as Lord in a secular society, that is a society in which many departments flourish in their own right, means that we must both be really inside them, aware of their own rules, and at the same time attentive to that 'Word' of God which is Jesus pronouncing his judgment upon all human living. When we have affirmed to the full the positive attitude towards human life which is implicit in a doctrine of creation through the logos of God, we must also recognise that this world is the one in which Jesus Christ was crucified. We shall consider at greater length in the next chapter the significance of the fact that Jesus was put to death by

[6] Cf. A. M. Ramsey, *Sacred and Secular* (Scott Holland Lectures, 1964; Longmans, 1965), p. 27. "It is easier to see the moral when we are looking back to the blunders of an earlier century than to apply it to the times in which we are living."

a combination of politics and religion which, in their own time, appeared to be very good specimens of politics and religion. 'The World' in the New Testament is an ambivalent expression. It means both the created order which God so loved that he entered into it and gave his son to die for it; it is at the same time human life organised in defiance of God, which could only result in the crucifixion of the incarnate Son of God. So our appreciation of the created world and the activity of God within it must always be controlled by our insight into the factors in the human situation which caused the crucifixion of goodness.

(c) To proclaim Jesus as Lord has a third consequence, a rediscovery of the universal sweep already present in New Testament thinking about the course of the world's history.

In John 1 : 1–5, 14 (N.E.B.) :

"When all things began, the Word already was. The Word dwelt with God, and what God was, the Word was. The Word, then, was with God at the beginning, and through him all things came to be; no single thing was created without him. All that came to be was alive with his life, and that life was the light of men. The light shines on in the dark, and the darkness has never mastered it."

"So the Word became flesh; he came to dwell among us, and we saw his glory, such glory as befits the Father's only Son, full of grace and truth."

In Col. 1 : 13–20 (N.E.B.) :

"He rescued us from the domain of darkness and brought us away into the kingdom of his dear Son, in

whom our release is secured and our sins forgiven. He
is the image of the invisible God; his is the primacy
over all created things. In him everything in heaven
and on earth was created, not only things visible but
also the invisible orders of thrones, sovereignties,
authorities, and powers: the whole universe has been
created through him and for him. And he exists before everything and all things are held together in
him. He is, moreover, the head of the body, the
church. He is its origin, the first to return from the
dead, to be in all things alone supreme. For in him
the complete being of God, by God's own choice,
came to dwell. Through him God chose to reconcile
the whole universe to himself, making peace through
the shedding of his blood upon the cross—to reconcile
all things, whether on earth or in heaven, through him
alone."

In Hebrews 1:1–4 (N.E.B.):

"When in former times God spoke to our forefathers,
he spoke in fragmentary and varied fashion through
the prophets. But in this the final age he has spoken
to us in the Son whom he has made heir to the whole
universe, and through whom he created all orders of
existence: the Son who is the effulgence of God's
splendour and the stamp of God's very being, and
sustains the universe by his word of power. When he
had brought about the purgation of sins, he took his
seat at the right hand of Majesty on high, raised as
far above the angels, as the title he has inherited is
superior to theirs."

In all these passages we have the reconciling of the
antithesis about which we have been speaking. Here is

the affirmation both that the logos, the meaning, the Word of God is the principle running right through creation and yet this world of God's making is the world in which his Son was crucified; but his crucifixion is itself the victory vindicated by his resurrection. In the end of the day, Christianity is profoundly optimistic. It is not a shallow optimism which pretends that evil and suffering do not exist. But it is optimistic in the sense that it believes that the last word lies with the goodness of God. The crucifixion is reminder enough that the passage of the world to its fulfilment is not a cheap, easy and automatic process. Suffering and sacrifice must be passed through on the way to glory. But it is the glory and not the suffering which is the last word. It is this conviction which enabled the English mystic in the fourteenth century, Dame Julian of Norwich, to proclaim with such simplicity. "All shall be well. All manner of things shall be well. All shall be well."[7] It is the same fundamentally Christian optimism which enables Teilhard de Chardin to see the final meaning of the long story of evolution in the Omega point which is the Christ.[8] There may be legitimate criticisms both of Teilhard's science and of his theology, but he is like the early map-makers, often wrong in the details but aware for the first time of whole new continents of experience to be accounted for. So let me conclude with this quotation from his meditation *The Mass on the World*.

[7] XIII Revelation of Divine Love, Warrack edition, p. 56.

[8] For those who have not yet been introduced to his thought I recommend the little paperback by Bernard Towers (*Teilhard de Chardin*, Lutterworth Press, 1968). I think it is better to start with a general introduction like this than to plunge right away into such difficult books as *The Phenomenon of Man*. The more mystical approach in *The Divine Milieu*, or perhaps even better his cosmic rhapsody *Hymn of the Universe* are better points at which to begin.

"Shatter, my God, through the caring of your revelation, the childishly timid outlook that can conceive of nothing greater or more vital in the world than the pitiable perfection of our human organism. On the road to a bolder comprehension of the universe the children of this world day by day outdistance the masters of Israel; but do you Lord Jesus 'in whom all things subsist', show yourself to those who love you as the higher Soul and the physical centre of your creation. Are you not well aware that for us this is a question of life or death? As for me, if I could not believe that your real Presence animates and makes tractable and enkindles even the very least of the energies which invade me or brush past me, would I not die of cold?

"I thank you, my God, for having in a thousand different ways led my eyes to discover the immense simplicity of things."

Alienation

But Thou wilt sinne and grief destroy;
That so the broken bones may joy.

George Herbert, *The Temple*

"Fings ain't what they used to be." Where does this sense come from that there is a gap between what is and what ought to be? Surely if we try to look at the business objectively and impartially, there is just as much a 'problem of good' as there is a problem of evil. What leads us to think that one state of affairs *ought* to be and that another state of affairs contradicts it? Is there any essential reason why we should think of life as a chequer board which is black with white squares on it rather than as a board which is white with black squares on it?

In the Hebrew–Christian tradition the problem arises because of the basic affirmation that the world is a good creation by a good Creator but that something is wrong. How it has 'gone wrong' is obviously a matter which can never be explained by any historical research for the contradiction in the situation goes as far back as knowledge itself. The traditional religious word for this condition of wrongness is sin. But let us take a different key word: *alienation*. It is a word which belongs more to the modern way of thinking than a good deal of the categories of sin and the mythology of the Fall. Dr. F. W. Dillistone in *The Christian Understanding of Atonement* begins by drawing attention to the fact that it is senseless to talk about the ideas behind such a word as atonement unless it presupposes a situation which has gone wrong and ought to be put right. He suggests that there are at any rate these four propositions of a general character which need to be accepted before the concept of 'alienation' can gain any kind of meaning. They are, Dr. Dillistone suggests:

1. That a distinctive creature exists that can be designated 'Man'. What precisely consitutes his distinctiveness—his capacity for self-transcendence or his ability to project himself through symbols—need not be debated in this context. All that matters is the agreement that there is one genus 'Man', and not a number of completely separable racial strains. There is a real entity that can be collectively described as humanity which is the creature aware of alienation.

2. That this creature is activated and motivated by numerous 'drives' which cry out for satisfaction.

3. That these instinctual drives can be thwarted and even dammed up, either by resistance from without or by negation from within.

4. That as a result of any such frustration which separates him from the goal of his desire man becomes alienated and is estranged and conscious of a malaise which he is seldom able to explain fully in rational terms.

So let us look at four areas in which this sense of alienation, of somehow having got separated from the fully satifactory, makes itself felt.

(a) *Man versus the universe.* C. S. Lewis began his book on *The Problem of Pain* by recollecting that as an atheist the reasons he would always have given for not believing Christianity were centred upon looking at the badness of creation as we all experience it. Bertrand Russell begins in the same vein in his book *Why I am not a Christian.* It *is* a fact that the universe as we know it contains things which we find offensive. It is not simply that it contains dangers and disasters which hurt, damage or destroy us. It is the fact that something deep down in us rebels against this being so. It is a fact, but it becomes a 'problem' when we see it as a contradiction of what ought to be. Man feels himself 'alienated' from the universe because, quite apart from what men do to each other, existence itself invites our moral revolt because of built-in features. It tells us something about the nature of Man himself that he has never been able to settle down to living in a universe that contains these features without trying to have some kind of explanation for them. From one point of view, all religions could be interpreted as human attempts to come to terms with our sense of alienation from the universe. We should go mad if we had no explanation to offer of the cruel, illogical, senseless elements which are experienced by just existing.

Broadly speaking there are three possible attitudes. One is 'monism' i.e. the assumption that God or ultimate reality or whatever name you care to give it, is itself beyond good and evil and however mysterious existence still remains, it is of the nature of reality that it should contain this unresolved contradiction and since we can't like it we must lump it. This is at least a response of the human spirit humbly to accept what is, in all its contradictoriness, because this is not simply cosmic lunacy but the nature of reality. A second possibility is 'dualism' i.e. the belief that reality contains within itself finally an unresolved and unresolvable conflict between good and evil. In such a system, whether primarily mythologised in terms of good spirits and evil spirits, devils and angels, or whether held in a more sophisti-

cated way in terms of a conflict of ideas, it offers to
men the challenge to align themselves with one side or
the other in the conflict, even though the conflict is itself
finally neither resolved nor resolvable. A third possibility, the one in which the Judeo-Christian tradition
stands, is to recognize that good is basic but that evil is
a reality and that in some way the good eventually
triumphs over the evil and has morally the last word.
But whatever label or -ism we attach to the attitude to
existence, the point remains that mankind universally
has been aware of contradiction and therefore of the
need, in order to preserve his sanity, to find some way
of projecting these experiences on to the universal
screen of existence itself.

(b) *Man in relation to society*. In addition to ex-
periencing some form of contradiction between himself
and the built-in features of the universe, Man is also
aware of his alienation from his fellow-men as organised in society. This takes many forms. A good example
is Karl Marx's definition of the way in which there is a
three-fold alienation of the worker from his work in a
capitalist system. It lies first of all in his economic
alienation in that he has no control over his raw material
and so cannot feel that he is truly identified with the stuff
which in his work he has to handle. Secondly, he is
alienated *sociologically* because he is isolated from his
fellow-men who are on the other side of the gulf separat-
ing the workers from the owners of raw material and
the means of production. Thirdly he is alienated *psycho-
logically* because work of this character excludes individual self-expression. All these factors lead, on the
Marxist analysis of society, by a highly complicated process of a dialectical kind to a condition of total alienation. This is one example of what is meant by blaming

alienation on to 'the System'. We are finding another contemporary expression of this in one aspect of student protest. Some of those who are most active in student unrest aim to bring about a destruction of 'the System' and the creation of another pattern in which alienation would not be necessary; they are following the same clue. Here 'the System' has brought about a breakdown in personal relationships and communication between the different elements that constitute university society.

Yet another burning issue in our time is the alienation between races which finds expression in violent racial conflict. Many would link this with various forms of blaming it on 'the System' e.g. that the racial conflict has come to be identified with the after-effects of the imperial system or the racial groups have come to be identified with class-conflicts in the capitalist system. One could give other examples, but the main feature of this approach to alienation is that it is in essence an awareness of conflict between the individual personality and some form of what we can almost call corporate personality. The individual feels helpless because he is aware of being gripped by something greater than himself and is aware that others, whom he would wish to be free to regard as individual personalities, are in their turn in the grip of a corporate personality which sets them as people over against him as a person. One of the frightening features of our own time is the wide areas of life which seem to be subject to just this kind of individual helplessness in the face of alienating forces. Incidentally, I believe that this is a perennial human experience which the New Testament mythologised in ways different from ours by talking of 'principalities and powers'. Man is not only alienated from the universal context of his existence but also alienated by finding himself caught up into corporate loyalties which are in conflict with other corporate loyalties. This is a double distress for it not only separates us from fellow-beings who are caught up into an antagonistic corporate loyalty (eg. workers *v.* employers) but sets us in antagonism to the corporate loyalty in which we find ourselves embroiled whether we like it or not in conflict with the other corporate loyalties (i.e. *because* I am a 'worker' I am, by definition 'alienated' from 'employers'). We can not get at our fellow-beings because we are both prisoners in our different camps.

(c) *Inter-personal alienation.* But is there also not an experience of alienation which can be felt even when there is no conflict between corporate loyalties? One of the interesting discoveries in the whole 'group dynamics' method is that all kind of conflicts tend to arise when persons who are not conscious of being caught up into group loyalties outside themselves are brought into inter-personal relationship, even on the scale of the quite small group. It is true that the conflicts which then reveal themselves may be, in part or perhaps wholly, explicable in terms of the backgrounds, assumptions and loyalties which each of us brings into the room when we come in. But the suggestion that this is entirely explicable in terms of group loyalties or corporate personality is belied by the fact that in the age-old experience of family life similar conflicts arise. Even if the perennial tension between parents and children is to be, at least in part, explained by their belonging respectively to different group-loyalties, we have still to account for the way in which the relationship between brothers and sisters in the same family or husband and wife of similar origins can lead to very bitter conflict. You do not need to be a trained marriage-guidance counsellor to know that much. It is interesting how much of modern writing, especially on the stage, is obsessed with this kind of conflict. Here again the tragic dimension is due to the fact that the conflicts are an undoubted fact of experience but they contradict the instinct of what ought to be. Plays like *Look Back in Anger* or *Who's Afraid of Virginia Woolf?* or the almost morbidly sensitive novels of Iris Murdoch are all studies in the alienation of persons from one another and yet they are given their power by the knowledge that some other kind of relationship ought to be possible.

(d) *Inner-personal alienation.* This again is an experience which is as old as human reflection upon selfhood. Paul in the seventh and eighth chapters of the Epistle to the Romans gives the classic New Testament interpretation of it. The plays of Shakespeare, supremely in the soliloquies of Hamlet, have fixed it in unforgettable verse. But the clinical analysis of it has dominated our age in the work of Freud. It is he who has invented the modern mythology for describing the self in using such frankly mythological expressions as the Oedipus-complex. For Freud, man is a creature who is moved by many instincts all of which are regulated by what he calls the 'pleasure principle'. As everybody knows, he has located in sexual desire the most powerful of the dominating impulses, giving to 'sexual' a far wider connotation than it normally has. But these powerful drives are never allowed free and unrestrained expression. There are many obstacles: physical conditions, social conventions and the religious taboos which have evolved in the course of human history. There are also certain internal factors which are the direct denial of the sexual life instincts, which he labelled the 'death instinct', directed against the ego and serving to increase the complexity of man's conscious and unconscious existence. The final outcome of the interaction of all these forces is a state of alienation in which the conscious is opposed to the unconscious, the super-ego to the ego, the death instincts to the life instincts, the wish-illusions to reality.[1] The resulting conditions of inner-alienation are described by a variety of labels, psychosis, neurosis, schizophrenia and other phrases which have passed into popular speech and journalism. The wards of the mental hospitals of the Western world are crowded with patients who are either well enough, at least at times, to describe themselves in such terms or are so described by their relations. We have never been so well equipped with words in which to describe the experience of inner-personal alienation though that seems to do little to contribute to the healing of it.

I am indebted to Dr. Dillistone's book for this four-fold division of the experience of alienation, man versus universe, man in relation to society, inter-personal alienation and inner-personal alienation. But, as the rest of his massive work makes clear, this is no more than a covenient classification to help understanding. The boundaries of each condition are ill-defined and their reactions upon each other are innumerable. It is obvious, for example, that a state of inner-personal alienation contributes powerfully to inter-personal alienation, e.g. in the form of conflict betwen man and wife, or parent and child. Inter-personal alienations quickly get mixed up with all those alienations which we try to blame on to 'the System'. The persons who find themselves in conflict with each other are never isolated individuals but are each the product of some kind of adherence to

[1] See F. W. Dillistone, *Christian Understanding of Atonement* (Nisbet, 1968), pp. 13–14.

a corporate loyalty, which may assume the compulsive proportions of a sense of being part of a corporate personality in conflict with other corporate personalities. The literature which is coming out of the civil rights conflict makes this clear. An individual American Negro who is in a state of inner-personal conflict is aware of belonging to a group-consciousness by virtue of his blackness which coincides with his alienation from other aspects of Western society because the blacks are the socially underprivileged. An alienation based on race can quickly pass over into an interpretation of alienation between man and the universe, so that the South African doctrine of apartheid is not merely a social and political doctrine but seeks to justify itself by an interpretation of race as a feature of creation.

The analysis hardly needs further elaboration. It may not be fashionable in non-religious circles to talk about sin, but there can be no doubt that the modern consciousness is deeply aware of the many forms which alienation can take. Has the terrific language in the Christian tradition about the significance of the death and resurrection of Jesus Christ really got anything to say to these undoubted facts of human experience?

The New Testament and the whole Christian tradition have borrowed phrases from all areas of man's experience to try to describe the relation between the death of Christ and the human awareness of alienation. For example there is the whole tradition which speaks in phrases like 'ransomed', 'bought with a price'. These take us back to old situations like slavery from which you can only be rescued if someone pays your master and so buys your freedom. Like a prisoner captured in war, or a victim caught by bandits, we can only be set free if someone comes along who puts down the ransom money and so delivers you from captivity. But, even if we have no personal experience of being in slavery or captured by bandits, we recognise that such metaphors are describing the experience which is one of the deadliest aspects of modern life, that we feel held, imprisoned by great powerful forces against which our tiny, feeble, individual wills are powerless. There is the terrifying growth of deadly armaments, nuclear and biological, everyone hating and fearing them, but no one apparently capable of taking the short, sensible step that we should throw them all away and be rid of them for ever. There is the mounting desperation of race conflict, so easy to denounce when you are outside any particular part of it like South Africa, but so quick to grow ugly and out of hand as soon as it begins to threaten our own standards of life, as it is beginning to do in certain parts of England. The generation which remembers the Nazis and the concentration camps has good reason to know that evil is not just a vacuum, an absence of good, but something active and powerful which gets hold of you and will not let you go. We have got into the wrong hands—and we are powerless to get out of them.

One of the ways in which the New Testament interprets this sense of being imprisoned is to speak of the 'principalities and powers' as the forces which get hold of mankind and subject us. This is part of the world picture (or mythology) in which the crucifixion of Jesus is interpreted, for example by St. Paul in Col. 2:13-15 (R.S.V.):

"And you, who were dead in trespasses and the uncircumcision of your flesh, God made alive together with him, having forgiven us all our trespasses, having cancelled the bond which stood against us with its legal demands; this he set aside, nailing it to the cross. He disarmed the principalities and powers and made a public example of them, triumphing over them in him."

This is splendid language—but what does it mean? How can we relate it to our experience? Here is set out, in all its richness, the proclamation that "GOD was in Christ". We can not make sense of the many-sided thought of atonement unless we hold together all the elements which come to a focus here. What are the essentials of that picture?

(1) God is a *good* Creator. Whatever may be wrong with the world as we know it, it does not have its origin in God. God is Christ-like and in Him is no unChrist-likeness at all. That is the central affirmation of all the resounding language in Col. 1—and found again in John 1 : 1–14 and Hebrews 1 (q.v. in N.E.B.). In Christ, we are let in on the character of God.

(2) But there is evil in the world. If it is not God's fault whose fault is it? Here we confront a logical dilemma—if God made us knowing that we should rebel, he is responsible. If he did not—he is not almighty. The nearest we can get to a solution is to say that he knew but reckoned it was worth it. In his overflowing love, he created *persons* who could have the joy of personal fellowship with their Creator. What could be better than that? Try to put together the best we can imagine of God—love, beauty, holiness—all that is good in our experience raised to infinite degree—and all the best we know of ourselves—capacity to know these good things and respond to them—and can you

imagine anything better? But it is built in to the whole
picture that it must be, from our side, a free response.
Anything other would be less than personal. So—if the
choice is free and real, it involves the possibility of
rejecting it. And the possible has happened—the offer
of communion with the divine has been refused. But the
possibility had to be there if the choice was to be personal and free.

(3) But why should it have to go wrong? It is con-
ceivable that free choice could have chosen bliss. We
only know that in fact we do not choose the best we
know. Why? Could it be because only infinite freedom
would infallibly choose the best and we are finite—not
infinite. So we could be misled in our choices or we
could be immature in our choices. Here the 'mytholo-
gies' try to picture the answer to 'why'—and both types
of answer are pictured.

(a) We are misled—the diversion comes from 'outside'
us—the serpent tempts Eve, who tempts Adam. (Is there
a primaeval anti-feminism there? Has it always been a
'man's world'?)

(b) We are immature—we mistake the choice and want
to be bigger than we are—"Let us be as gods . . ."

Subsequent Christian thought contains both strains—
on the whole, the West follows Augustine in emphasising the disobedience; the East follows Irenaeus in
emphasising the immaturity, at least in the sense that the
meaning of human history lies in a movement towards
perfection (theosis).

Frankly, it is here that I personally find it hardest to
reconcile being a man of the Christian tradition and
being a man of the modern world. I do not know precisely how nineteen centuries of Christian thought
actually *felt* about Adam—but all the language treats

him as an historical figure, comprising in himself the whole potentiality of the human race. 'The seed of Adam' is used literally to describe all subsequent humanity. "As in Adam all die" (I Cor. 15:22) is a realistic shorthand to describe the mortality of all men. And so the N.T., the Fathers and all theology down to the mid-nineteenth century is able to *feel* a real antithesis between the 'Old Adam', alienated by rebellion against God and Christ the 'New Adam', reconciled to God because he is humanity in total obedience to his Father.

But we can no longer think wholeheartedly in that way. We know little of the actual process by which hominids, the most developed form of the primates, became *homo sapiens*. Anthropologists differ in their definition of where the transition can be located. There are tool-using apes. It is hard to say where animal communication becomes speech, or even when self-reflection begins. Certainly, by the time you get to cave paintings you have the characteristically human exercise of communication through symbols. But was there ever an 'unfallen man', i.e. a man who was conscious of moral choice but did not in fact deliberately disobey his conscience? Or did the emergence of moral sense coincide with its misuse? And what is 'moral sense' at this level? The primitive instincts are directed towards such necessary ends as the survival of the individual or of the group. Was the first 'sinner' the primitive man who chose a course of action which he thought was to *his* advantage though against the interests of the tribe? If so—he can not have persisted in it too far or he would not have survived. If he did survive, can his choice have been 'wrong' when his survival led to further evolution? At this point, I get lost! But how much does it matter?

Do we need to posit any kind of 'historic fall' so long as we hold on to the two main points of the biblical myth, viz.

(a) that the creation, including man, is in the intention of the Creator *good*;

(b) that Man, as we know ourselves to be part of that species, is aware of a contradiction between himself and the rest of existence which he feels ought not to be there. The awareness of being in that condition is, in Christian shorthand, sin.

This seems to me to be a sufficient description of the known facts—and there I am content to leave it.

(4) *Into that situation comes Christ.* Call him the 'second Adam' if that helps to distinguish him from the rest of the human situation. But the essential point is that here is a Man in whom the contradiction is transcended. Here there is no gap between what IS and what OUGHT to be. But another contradiction asserts itself. The consequence of there being no conflict between what IS and what OUGHT is the conflict in which what IS destroys what OUGHT. Christ is crucified. The Son of Man must suffer. The gospel—the 'good news'—is that the attempted destruction failed. God raised Christ from the dead. The attempted destruction of what OUGHT to be by what IS fails when the OUGHT is united with what IS in the risen Christ, who is 'alive for evermore'.

Let us try to see whether that way of putting it speaks meaningfully to the four-fold alienation (see pp. 44–50). 1. *Man versus the universe.* If *God* was in Christ, then the cross and resurrection of Christ says something about the nature of reality. It still does not provide a logical, intellectual answer to 'the problem of evil'. But it does demonstrate that God himself enters into the arena of evil and suffering and, through a total self-giving in love, is hurt to the death, yet beyond that death is known as still alive. To share in that suffering love is to know in ourselves the reconciliation, the atonement, with the whole universe. Language falters, because the words are cheap, unconvincing, without the experience. But I recently came across some words of Simone Weil, the Jew who never formally became a Christian and who starved herself to death in 1942 because she insisted on taking no more than the rations of her fellow-beings in the concentration camps of occupied France. "Affliction is a nail driven into our souls, fastening us to the very centre of the Universe . . ." at "the point of intersection, between creation and Creator, which is also the point of intersection of the two branches of the Cross". Christ "conquered the world simply because He, being the truth, continued to be the Truth in the very depth of extreme affliction".[2] That speaks with the authority of one who has known suffering.

2. *Man alienated in society*—perhaps the words become a little more meaningful as we move in from the universal to the social. St. Paul interprets the cross as a victory over 'the principalities and powers' (see p. 47 above). We may re-mythologise (i.e. re-interpret) this idea in terms of the corporate-personalities, the forces ouside ourselves which capture and control us. Perhaps this can be made more vivid if we picture the crucifixion of Jesus in terms of a conspiracy between politics and religion to destroy him. Roman politics and Jewish religion were very good examples of their kind. Roman politics were just, ordered, comprehensive—by any standard. Jewish religion was devout, disciplined, gen-

---

[2] Simone Weil, *On Science, Necessity and the Love of God*, translated by R. Rees (Oxford University Press, 1968), reviewed by Malcolm Muggeridge in the *Observer*, March 2nd 1968.

erous—all that the vicar's Lenten letter in the parish
magazine urges you to be. Yet, as we read the Passion
narrative we see how each became *demonic*—in the
sense that the individual actors are progressively pos-
sessed by the corporate loyalty that binds them. Pilate
struggles *not* to condemn Jesus—but his job is to keep
order or prevent a riot; Herod is reconciled to Pilate—
but at the price of ganging up with him against Jesus.
Caiaphas and the Sanhedrin are genuinely concerned to
suppress blasphemous heresy and the High Priest, mix-
ing religion with politics, reaches the reasonable con-
clusion that it is better that one man should die than that
the whole people perish. The soldiers and the crowds
tag along—no more brutal by their standards than
soldiers often are, no more fickle than a demonstration
in Grosvenor Square.

What atonement does suffering love offer to man
alienated in society? It is essential to honesty that we
should not, at this point, take refuge in abstractions—
a sort of Tolstoyan renunciation of politics or a spurious
'spiritualisation' of religion. All history proves at least
that you can not live outside history. The pacifist leaves
someone else to rule and the perfectionist creates his
own sect. The way of the cross in politics and religion
is something more ambiguous and more apparently
tragic which can be summarised as *living by forgiveness*.
In politics, it is Cromwell staking everything politically
upon the execution of Charles I whilst crying to Parlia-
ment "I beseech you, in the bowels of Christ, think it
possible you may be mistaken": in religion, it is recog-
nising that part of the victory of Martin Luther was
Ignatius Loyola; in both, it is Martin Luther King leading passive resistance to the point where he was shot.
In short, it is doing what you believe to be *right* in the

social situation in which you are imprisoned with a
depth of love for your opponent imprisoned in *his* social
situation which sets you both free to meet a God who is
not imprisoned in either of your situations.

3. *Inter-personal alienation*—we must again face a
paradox. Jesus was essentially a reconciler of persons
and his clue was forgiveness. Nothing is deeper in his
teaching than that only forgivers can be forgiven. He
embedded that teaching in the prayer which all Christians say more often than any other. Yet equally deep in
his teaching is the awareness that he himself would be
the cause of deep division between people, even those
naturally closest. "I have come to set a man against
his father, a daughter against her mother . . . a man
will find his enemies under his own roof." (Mat. 10:35–
36, N.E.B.)

Again, the paradox is resolved only in the nature of
suffering love. Christ *divides* when he calls us to follow
the way of suffering love. To refuse that way is to be
alienated from each other. To accept it is to die—and
thereby to be reunited with each other. To forgive even
a little is to die a little; to forgive completely is to die
completely.

H. R. Mackintosh, in *The Christian Experience of
Forgiveness* puts this truth movingly:

"We are constantly under a temptation to suppose
that the reason why we fail to understand completely
the atonement made by God in Christ is that our
minds are not sufficiently profound. And doubtless
there is truth in the reflection that for final insight
into the meaning of the Cross we are not able or
perspicacious enough. But there is a deeper reason
still. It is that we are not good enough; we have never

forgiven a deadly injury at a price like this, at such cost to ourselves as came upon God in Jesus' death . . . Let the man be found who has undergone the shattering experience of pardoning, nobly and tenderly, some awful wrong to himself, still more to one beloved by him, and he will understand the meaning of Calvary better than all the theologians of the world."

Such an experience, costingly known in our dealings with each other, illuminates as nothing else can the truth that only one who was good enough to forgive utterly would be able to break the barrier which keeps us, who need to be forgiven as he never did, from the forgiving which is the condition of forgiveness. Mrs. Alexander, (that great Doctor of the Church) expressed it with disarming simplicity in her children's hymn—

> "There was no other good enough
> To pay the price of sin.
> He only could unlock the gate
> Of heaven—and let us in."

4. *Inner-personal alienation.* We, in this post-Freudian age, have never been so well equipped with a vocabulary to describe our inner conflicts, but we are not for that reason noticeably nearer to resolving them. I do not for one moment want to suggest ingratitude for all that modern science, especially psychiatric medicine, can do to heal disordered personality. We need only to reflect on the sufferings of the mentally ill even a century ago to be deeply grateful for all the skill and compassion that go into alleviating the deep distresses of the torn self. I wrote this passage after listening to a day's debate in the House of Lords on the care and after-care of

prisoners. There Christians and humanists alike exhibited a deep and sensitive awareness of the plight of those whose inner distress has caused their alienation from society. We know much more about the extent to which people are not to be blamed for states which early conditioning especially have created and which can never be wholly cured. Surely the basis of such compassion is the recognition, however one would word it, that "There, but for the grace of God, go I". We are *all* wounded in our psyche: we are all divided persons. We can none of us claim that it is *our* credit that we have not been locked up for it.

One of the effects that Jesus had upon people was to make them see that more clearly. "Depart from me, for I am a sinful man, O Lord." It is a universal characteristic of the saints that the clearer their vision of God, the sharper the sense of their own unworthiness. Yet it is of the essence of the New Testament meaning of the word 'saint' that it is to know you are a forgiven sinner. The heart of forgiveness is to know that one is accepted. The death of Jesus is the deepest possible exhibition of the cost of forgiveness and the strongest possible assurance that the cost has been paid. When the risen Christ returned in forgiveness to the disciples who had deserted him and fled, there the Church was born. It is the universal testimony of Christians down the ages—witnessed to in the pages of the New Testament and echoed by millions, in liturgies and hymns and prayers, that nowhere like the foot of the cross can it be seen that God accepts us as we are—and that life starts again from there. "If God is for us, who *can* be against us? . . . It is Christ, Christ who died, and more than that was raised from the dead, who is at God's right hand and indeed pleads our cause. Then what *can* separate us from the love of Christ?" Nothing, nothing at all.

Once more it is suffering love which is the clue. And the greater the love, the deeper the suffering. We know it in our own experience. Only love for those whose inner division separates them from their fellows can hope to win them back again. The deeper the division within them, the more patient and persistent must be the love that woos them back into relationship. In Christ crucified we see the depth of the love, 'Christ crucified until the end of time', which deals in unbreakable persistence with our broken selves, accepting us, as we are until we want to be as He is.

There is a poem, written by the late Dorothy Sayers when she was still an Oxford undergraduate, which expresses vividly the resistance by our divided self to such costly loving—and the final surrender to it.

> Go, bitter Christ, grim Christ; haul if thou wilt
> Thy bloody cross to thine own bleak Calvary.
> When did I bid thee suffer for my guilt
> To bind intolerable claims on me?
> I loathe thy sacrifice; I am sick of thee.
>
> They say thou reignest from thy cross. Thou dost,
> And like a tyrant. Thou dost rule by tears,
> Thou womanish son of woman. Cease to thrust
> Thy sordid tale of sorrows in my ears,
> Jarring the music of my few short years.
>
> I am battered and broken and weary and out of
>   heart,
> I will not listen to talk of heroic things,
> But be content to play some simple part

Freed from preposterous, wild imaginings.
Men were not made to walk as priests and kings.

Thou liest, Christ, thou liest! Take it hence
That mirror of strange glories. I am I;
What wouldst thou make of me? O cruel pretence,
Drive me not mad so with the mockery
Of that most lovely, unattainable lie.

O king, O Captain, wasted, wan with scourging,
Strong beyond speech and wonderful with woe,
Whither, relentless, wilt thou still be urging
Thy maimed and halt, that have not strength to go?
Peace, peace, I follow. Why must we love thee so?

Contact

By all means use sometimes to be alone.
Salute thyself: see what thy soul doth wear.

George Herbert, *The Temple*

When the Beatles sought to learn meditation, having flooded the world with the exuberance of their sound, they went to India, to the ashram of the Maharishi. It was a parable of our age. First, in the day of the transistor, silence is a treasure to be sought. Second, it never occurs to the typical products of Western culture that our own tradition contains an ancient, coherent and sublime tradition of mysticism. It is assumed that one must go to the East to seek the contemplative life. There is great confusion of mind as to what mysticism is, a confusion exhibited in the controversy about the psychedelic experience induced by drugs and its relationship to what the Christian tradition means by mystical states. The former is sought as an end in itself and has no relation to moral will: the latter have always been an unsought by-product of union with the source of moral holiness. But the Western mystical tradition has lost any authority it ever had and the goal of well-publicised world-renunciation lies somewhere in the mysterious East.

Yet the hunger is real. The Beatles represented the best of their generation not only in their vitality but in their compassion; their insight into human loneliness, their frustration by the generation gap—all this throbs

in their music. But *really* to care is to start asking
questions whose answer is blowing in the wind.

There is a hunger for the things which religion is
meant to answer—but there is a great doubt as to what
kind of religion answers them. It is a doubt which the
religious share. Among Christians, traditional 'spirituality' is much under question.[1]

Yet we can not let the matter alone. For years an
unlikely book was a best seller in the U.S.A., *Elected
Silence* by Thomas Merton, a Trappist monk; in England, the 'religious' life of monks and nuns causes a
puzzled fascination to the popular mind on television
and in coloured-supplement journalism. Ours is a profoundly religious age—at least in the sense in which St.
Paul found the Athenians religious. Acts 17:22 in the
old Authorised Version has Paul saying bluntly: "I
perceive that in all things ye are too superstitious". In
the New English Bible this has become: "I see that in
everything that concerns religion you are uncommonly
scrupulous". The modern mood ranges across all that
either translation might describe.

"Where *is* God to be found today." It is often an
agonisingly sincere question, behind the easy and unselfconscious discussion of religion which one may have
in any bar or waiting-room. It was one of the benefits
of *Honest to God* that it made the public discussion of
religion as respectable as the public discussion of sex.[2]

[1] See e.g. *Spirituality for Today*, ed. E. James (S.C.M. Press,
1968), the report of a conference at Durham in August 1967, in
which every aspect of private and liturgical prayer comes under
fire—including the validity of monasticism.

[2] And it is as significant that Dr. John Robinson's book which
followed, though not so immensely popular, should be called *Exploration into God* (S.C.M. Press, 1967) and be much concerned
with mysticism.

But the urgency lies in the *today*. The Church seems forever to be talking of the past, to be sending us back two thousand years to start with Jesus. How do you make contact *now*? That is to introduce another aspect of the way in which Christianity seeks to answer man's questions—the Holy Spirit.

It may seem that the Holy Spirit is dragged in at this point to fit a preconceived pattern. But that is only true in the sense that from very early times when Christians wanted to speak of how the God and Father of Jesus Christ continues to be active here and now, 'Holy Spirit' is the phrase they used. Yet the Holy Spirit is in some ways the most unreal and the most real aspect of the Godhead as Christians think of him. The third person of the Godhead is unreal partly because of the vagueness of the pictorial images which we can have of the Spirit. Whether they are helpful or not, the images we associate with God the Father are at any rate meaningful. The very word 'Father', like the words 'King' and 'Sovereign,' call up ideas and realities with which we are familiar. When we speak of the second person of the Trinity we are speaking of a man who is at least vividly portrayed in the Gospels. But there can be no comparable concreteness in our calling up of all possible images of the Holy Spirit in architecture and art. We do our best with doves, flames and representations of the wind. We feel at a loss in seeking to make the Holy Spirit vivid.

There is a sense in which it is hard to see the Holy Spirit precisely because he is the power by which we see at all.

This is why, in another sense, he is the most real; because he is the author of all knowledge of good and of God. As the hymn puts it 'Every virtue we possess and every victory won, and every thought of holiness are His alone'. It is the nature of the Holy Spirit to lead away from himself, and yet truly to lead. He has an incurable tendency to self-effacement. But if it is true that the Holy Spirit, for all our difficulties in picturing him, is in fact known in all the ways in which we find ourselves linked with God, then to speak of the Holy Spirit is inevitable at this stage in our discussion. He links us with God in a variety of ways.

First there is all that immediacy of knowledge and experience of God of which Christian history and our knowledge of Christians today continually speak. Of course it always seems possible to think of some alternative explanation, but you can not get away from the fact that men and women are greatly changed; that strange experiences called 'conversion' have taken place; that there are in men's minds experiences of that magic leap like the electric power which flashes from point to point of an arc-lamp bringing light between two separate objects, that experience by which the things of 2,000 years ago in the New Testament become consuming realities of present experience. It is not about those that I am primarily concerned here but they are one area in which Christians affirm that the Holy Spirit is alive and real and do so in the face of all the attempts to find an alternative explanation.

There is a second great area in which the Holy Spirit is known, by his indwelling the Body of Christ, the Church. But what we mean by talking of that is going to be our subject in a later chapter.

Thirdly there is another whole area generally called *prayer* and *worship*, and that is the mode of contact with God which we begin to explore now.

PRAYER

For purposes of this discussion, we mean by prayer
that personal communication, or at least the search for
communication, between each one of us and God. If
that is what we are talking about, two points seem
clear: that prayer is important and that prayer is difficult.

Is it important? There was a book published at the
time when I was a theological student, which made a
lasting impression on me, called *The Art of Mental
Prayer* by Dom Bede Frost and it begins "To pray and
to teach souls to pray, it is all; for given this everything
else will follow". And there is no doubt that many
priests of my generation and older grew up to believe
that this is central to our lives and to our priestly
responsibilities. We still believe that and still try to do
it. But we are well aware of the changed climate, of the
way in which questions are being asked in a new way.
There is need for more simplicity in the practising and
the teaching of prayer and many of the manuals about
prayer, which so many of us have so hopefully bought
one after the other, have proved so inadequate. And yet
I would still affirm that prayer is important, for at least
three reasons—one negative and two positive.

Negatively, if you do not pray you are left with a
suspicion that at the heart of yourself there is a gap
which you have not dared to face. To attempt to pray
is to unlock your haunted room at the centre of the
mansion of the soul. It is the locked door you face when
you are left in silence, when you are left in solitude,
and the man who does not pray is a haunted man—
haunted by uncertainty as to what is behind that locked
door. What shall we find if we open it? Is there some-

one in there with whom we must come to terms? Or is he someone who is not so much an unknown guest in the house as an unknown master who, if you let him out, will claim the rule of the whole house? He might be mad, a gibbering idiot, stark, staring mad. Can we afford not to know? Some suspect that he is mad; and that at the heart of ourselves there is madness. Is that what the suicides feared to find? May God have mercy on their souls for who can guess what it is like to believe that *that* is what you find within the secret room. And there are others who have opened it and found it empty— there is no one there—nothing, nothing at all. And then what? There is nothing in the secret room at all—then any meaning the mansion of the soul may have is a meaning you must yourself provide, for no one else will. This is the courage of the atheist. This is the dignity and the integrity of a Jean-Paul Sartre or an Albert Camus, the atheist whose prayer is to come to final terms with himself for there is nothing else to come to terms with. To read for example Camus' novel *The Plague* is to deepen immeasurably one's appreciation of the sheer integrity that is needed to be open to prayer in a Godless world. These are the sort of doubts about what is in the inner room that lie on each side of the knife-edge of faith. Because faith asks "Is there someone there who responds, answers, claims the whole house for his own?" And one is glad, so glad, that he should do so. Can we afford not to know?

Secondly and positively, Jesus prayed. Part of the unmistakable portrait that emerges from the gospels is the Jesus who faced the true wilderness and the struggles of temptation that awaited him there; the Jesus who arose a great while before dawn; who prepared in long prayer for choosing the twelve; who escaped into the mountain-side from the throngs clamouring to be healed; who sweated blood in prayer in the garden whilst his disciples slept—if Jesus is all that we have claimed for him, to be a proper man is to seek the Heavenly Father in prayer. To call God *Abba*, Father, is to want, or at least to need, to pray. Central to what Jesus left us is all that followed from his saying to his disciples "When you pray say Abba, Father, who art in heaven". No one can pretend to follow Jesus and not see that prayer is important because it is part of him.

The third reason follows simply from that. There is no doubt that there has always been a connection between the effectiveness of his followers and their life in prayer. It is at this point that we become aware of that immense, vital, varied heritage of the past masters of prayer. And this is where the priest and many a lay person [3] too, has, with the priest, a responsibility to know something of their heritage and to help it to come alive for others.

Why is that tradition not alive amongst us and why do you and I find prayer difficult? Even when we know prayer is important, why do we find it difficult?

There are some obvious answers. The first might be taken from the title of that book of Bede Frost *The* Art *of Mental Prayer*, for all art is difficult to master. We know that perfectly well, but to speak of prayer as an art is after all only an analogy, not a complete description. For prayer is also surely something spontaneous, something natural. The inevitable and natural response of love to love. Though even here, there is an element of art, because people do properly speak of the art of

---

[3] We remember in recent history Von Hugel and Evelyn Underhill, Olive Wyon and C. S. Lewis.

friendship, or the art of lovemaking. Yet there is a difference. Here the analogies are best drawn from love and friendship to illustrate the transformation of personality that is involved. When I consider what God is like and then what I am like, I need not be surprised that a good deal needs to be done to me before I am able to be at home in prayer. That is why the classical tradition always contained the note of purifying, *askesis*, the traditional sequence, the three-fold way, of purgation, illumination, union.

Another explanation of why we find prayer difficult certainly lies in trying to force oneself into an unsuitable pattern. People do have much in common, that is the basis of general schemes and traditions. But people also greatly vary. As Dom John Chapman, another great teacher of prayer was constantly repeating 'pray as you can and don't try to pray as you can't'. I have always been greatly helped by a three-fold distinction which Von Hugel makes in *The Mystical Element in Religion*. The three elements to which he draws attention are (1) the intellectual or theological, (2) the historical or liturgical and (3) the mystical or intuitive. Those three elements are always to be found together in the fullness of religion, and any given individual is likely to find himself in sympathy with one or another of them more than the others as his natural starting place; growth in the Christian life is not only to grow in that which is natural to you but to learn to grow in the unfamiliar too.

The intellectual-theological type of praying is the most familiar and was the main tradition from at any rate the seventeenth century until quite recently. It is as old as Christianity; it is splendidly expressed, richly mixed with other ingredients, in St. Augustine's

Confessions. It gets its classical exposition in books like the *Spiritual Exercises* of Ignatius Loyola; it is well expressed in the great French seventeenth-century teachers of prayer; it lies at the basis of all that conception of meditation which consists, as somebody once put it, of preaching yourself a sermon. It is the way of approach which uses the mind as the means of ascent into God.

Secondly there is the kind of prayer and the kind of pray-er more at home, not with abstract ideas, but with the concrete things of history and the corporate experiences of the liturgy. Liturgy can be understood in a very wide sense to cover all that kind of prayer which, even when you are praying alone, is very dependent upon the sense of companionship with others. Liturgy can be either the ancient liturgical traditions of the Eastern or Western Church or the spontaneity and companionship of the prayer meeting, or the kind of praying, especially intercession, which is most at home in thinking about *people*.

Thirdly there is the mystical-intuitive approach, less dependent upon words and often quite independent of them. It is not easily expressed corporately, except in the great attempt which the tradition of the Society of Friends illustrates. It has its unbroken exponents down the Christian ages and is warmly and vividly expressed in our English tradition in that group of mystical writers of the fourteenth century including Walter Hilton, Richard Rolle of Hampole, the author of *The Cloud of Unknowing* and, warmest and most vivid of them all to my mind, Mother Julian of Norwich in *The Showings of Divine Love*.

Each of us may start to pray in the way which comes most naturally to us and be glad of whatever reality and spontaneity is there given. But let us also be sufficiently aware of the grand dimensions of the Christian Temple to know that there are undiscovered treasures to be enjoyed and vistas which, having brought joy to others, may yet delight us too.

WORSHIP

In this context I use the word to mean public and liturgical prayer. Much of what has been said about personal and private prayer applies again—but liturgical worship has both advantages and disadvantages of its own. It has all the strengths which derive from being corporate, objective, venerable—and the corresponding weaknesses.

On the credit side, is to be set the exhilaration which has come to much of Christendom through the renewal of public worship, including the fresh light on the meaning of Scripture which has been shed by the new translations. But the debit side of the same phenomenon is a widespread dismay and distress.

Perplexed Christians may take these two big and balancing thoughts to ponder.

(a) We are called to live through a difficult period of self-consciousness in worship. This is dangerously destructive of the heart of worship itself, but is yet unavoidable. Every civilisation is far more dependent than it realises, until it loses them, upon certain accepted emotions, attitudes and ideas which everybody takes for granted. These get focussed into words and all that words symbolise, like fatherhood, kingship, liberty, democracy, patriotism. If you like to continue this exercise for yourself, draw up a list in the family, each one separately, of the seven most significant words you can think of. And then see how your lists compare with each other. What happens in times of great cultural revolution is that people's lists come to have much less in common.

Such periods of cultural revolution hit religion particularly hard. More perhaps than any form of corporate activity, it depends upon people having the same emotional responses to the same words and symbols.

At a recent meeting of the World Council of Churches we not only had all the problems that arise from confessional unfamiliarity, e.g. the way in which an American Baptist finds it hard to understand the worship of the Russian Orthodox, but also some demonstrations of modern forms of music and worship which only made it clear that none of us is at home in any one form of words and acts at all. This is perhaps the hardest of all ways in which practising Christians to-day have to learn to live with change.

So liturgical revision is of a piece with the revolution that is going on in all the arts, whether of stage, cinema, poetry, painting or anything else. It is the Church's recognition that the things which move men are changing. No one can tell how long it will be before in the arts generally, or in liturgy in particular, we are able to discover an unselfconscious community of values and symbols, in which we can loose ourselves in communion with the thing symbolised rather than be left in awareness of the symbols.

Our job in the Church, as a whole, is a more modest one of ensuring that liturgy changes enough to make clear that it is a living organism and not a dead fossil and that it echoes with greater faithfulness what actually moves us in our minds and lives.

(b) All this is taking place in a recovery as wide as Christendom of a fresh understanding of the sacramental nature of the Church. Nowhere has this found a better and more biblical expression than in the *Constitution on the Church* of the Second Vatican Council. In the very first paragraph it proclaims "The Church is, in Christ, the sacrament of the unity of all men with God and with one another".

Worship is a deep human need. We are trustees for something men need to keep them fully human. It is as though the whole organisation of the world was a vast complex of reinforced concrete, with the Church like the wire mesh running right through the whole fabric giving it strength. Within the Church itself, a living network of sacraments holds the frame together. No inorganic image will suffice, it is rather that here are the living muscles and blood vessels of the body.

It is as we increasingly see the vital part which sacraments play in the common life of the Body of Christ that we shall see the point of liturgical revision and find it worth while.

Let us pray that we may learn new relationships, where need be, in the Church at a time when many feel sadly bewildered by the pace of change. Let us picture Mary Magdalene in the garden of the resurrection, as she had to learn to leave the familiar relationship with Jesus as she had known him, and find a new one.

IMAGES: —A PRAYER

O Christ, my Lord, again and again I have said with Mary Magdalene, "They have taken away my Lord and I know not where they have laid him". I

have been desolate and alone. And thou has found me
again, and I know that what has died is not thou, my
Lord, but only my idea of thee, the image which I
have made to preserve what I have found, and to be
my security. I shall make another image, O Lord,
better than the last. That, too, must go, and all successive images, until I come to the blessed vision of
thyself, O Christ, my Lord.[4]

[4] George Appleton, *One Man's Prayers* (S.P.C.K., 1967).

The Shame and the Glory of the Church

And now in age I bud again,
After so many deaths I live and write,
I once more smell the dew and rain,
And relish versing: O my onely light,
It cannot be
That I am he
On whom thy tempests fell all night.

George Herbert, *The Temple*

The child who said, "I love Jesus but I hate God" was reflecting, with childish directness, the dilemma which many feel when contrasting the Old Testament with the New. "I love Jesus but I hate the Church" reflects a love-hate relationship to Mother Church which many people to-day also feel. We are well aware of the bad patches in the old lady's past record. We tend to divide into shamed embarrassment or malicious glee at the remembrance of the Inquisition or the case of Galileo. We are aware of the reproach that no wars have been so bloody as the wars of religion. On top of all this, those of us who live in and love the Church of our upbringing, are only too well aware of the ways in which it fails to measure up to the demands of the present age. It is true that in all parts of Christendom, including the Church of England, some strenuous efforts are being made to bring the Church into the twentieth century before it is over. We watch with admiration the efforts of the Roman

Catholic Church to bring about what Pope John had in mind when he spoke of *aggiornamento*. It simply means 'bringing up to date', the attempt to remould the Church so that it is more relevant to the rapidly changing pattern of the modern world. This is a heartbreakingly slow business. It causes great distress among those who have come to love the Church in which they grew up. Human nature by and large seems to be averse to change and religious human nature often seems more averse than any other. I think that the hardest lesson I have learned as a bishop is the toughness of the material out of which institutions are made. The amount of spiritual and intellectual energy which has to be generated before one cubic foot of institutional life can be changed seems to be prodigious. Some thirty years ago I was enlisted by my then bishop, Dr. Leslie Hunter of Sheffield, in the campaign which he was leading under the title of 'Men, Money and the Ministry'. Many of the courses which he advocated then are now at last on the agenda in such documents as the Morley Report *Partners in Ministry*. Those of us who were involved in the long and too-often tedious business of Church Assembly and Convocation realise with sinking hearts how much time and energy is needed to stay where we are, let alone to advance.

Behind this dissatisfaction with the Church as an institution, there lies a deeper question. Does the religion of Jesus, with all its spontaneity, human freshness, compassionate concern with people and readiness to challenge the accepted conventions of the day, really demand the ponderous and inflexible machinery which seems to be associated with the organised Church? This is no new question. One of the sad ironies of Church history is the way in which movements which set out to give freshness and flexibility to the Church seem, in their turn, to generate fresh institutions, which become as in-flexible and as irrelevant as those which they sought to replace. Such attempts raise acutely the question of whether the Church can ever be renewed without caus-ing fresh splits and whether the effect of renewal move-ments is not simply to multiply the institutional barriers to freedom and spontaneity of the spirit.

But alongside this scepticism about whether Jesus ever intended to found a Church at all, has appeared a more recent approach which calmly assumes that the Christian religion is likely to need a sociological mani-festation since sociological manifestations are part of all enterprises of the human spirit. There are many books which examine the Church as one social institution among others. Sometimes these are written with the impartiality of the professional sociologist.[1] Others are no less professional and detached in approach as in the case of David Martin[2] or Peter Rudge[3] but they are written by people inside the organised Church and even in its ordained ministry but with sociological training. Sometimes the combination of theological with socio-logical jargon makes the style even more unreadable than either jargon separately. But I at least have learned theological lessons from fresh insights into how the Church functions as a social phenomenon, just as one gets from psychology fresh insights into what makes oneself function as an individual person. It may do little to contribute towards the solving of problems beyond the help, not inconsiderable, of getting clearer what the problems are.

There are two aspects of the Church as a sociological

---

[1] Like Bryan Wilson, *Religion in Secular Society* (Watts, 1966).

[2] *The Sociology of English Religion* (S.C.M. Press, 1967).

[3] *Ministry and Management* (Tavistock Publications, 1968).

fact which are of interest before we turn to ask whether
the Church as founded by Jesus Christ does anything
to answer the need to which they point.

(a) Identity

There is an intriguing little book by F. B. Welbourn [4]
about *identity* as the problem which the modern African
faces when his traditional tribal and cultural patterns
break up and the new pattern has not yet taken its place.
What is being pointed to is simply the human need to
belong. We all belong to various groups and if anything
happens to make us feel separated from them we lose
our nerve and begin to wonder who we are. Fundamentally the family is the basic unit of belonging. We are
tragically aware of the inability to fit anywhere else into
society which overtakes those who have never had a
family to which they felt they could belong. Unless the
earliest years, even those before conscious memory begins, can establish the sense that the individual is sur-
rounded by a community which accepts him as he is and
values him not for any achievements but simply because
he is there, then nothing else can establish the needed
sense of self-respect over against society at large.
Modern educationalists appreciate vividly the opportunity which school affords in the next stage. Here the
small circle of the family begins to widen out and a great
deal of the contemporary argument, for example about
the virtues of independent schools or of the Comprehensive system, is an argument about whether these provide the right kind of extension of experience of identity
as found within the family. In later life we begin to
belong to a variety of other communities of shared values.

[4] *Religion and Politics in Uganda* (East African Publishing
House, 1965).

The Women's Institute or the Trade Union branch or the professional association or even the bowling club and the local pub become manifestations of 'belonging' in one or another aspect of our personality. For many people the local church is simply one form of the fulfilment of this need and nothing more. It would be perfectly possible to have a quite rewarding relationship to the local church which did not need to involve any experience of God at all. There is an advertisement which I pass frequently which says 'You can be very lonely in London. If you are, join this church'. Fair enough, and it is good as far as it goes. And the minister could always reply that anybody having joined for that very human reason might well come into relationship with God afterwards. But by the same token a good deal of the criticism of the Church is that it is no more than a religious club or (even more derogatory) a 'Christian Ghetto'.

A second aspect of the sociological approach has to do with *universality*. Marshall Macluhan has made us aware of the way in which the modern media of communication have turned this world into a 'global village'. In the electronic age, the instantaneous nature of coexistence has created a state of affairs in which we are all as immediately aware of each other on a world-wide scale as used to be true only in the village community. But it is a distorted awareness in that it is the tragedy, the violence, the horror which attracts attention. So the nearness breeds its own reaction. Racism, the extravagances of apartheid, the growth of regionalism, the exuberant patriotism of the newly independent Afro-Asian nations are all the other side of the universal community to which we know we can not escape belonging, but which denies our deepest needs as much as it satisfies them.

The Church has always had this ambiguous paradoxical, dialectic character—which is only to say that as soon as you have said one thing about it, you have to correct the balance by saying something else. In the New Testament, the Church is always a collection of sinning saints, of sanctified sinners just as, in its roots in the Israel of the Old Testament, it is always God's chosen people and the object of withering denunciation by the prophets. The paradox runs right through, so that you can never be sure whether the Church is being blasted for being too little like Jesus Christ or for being too much like him.

The Christian Church has its roots in the Old Testament.

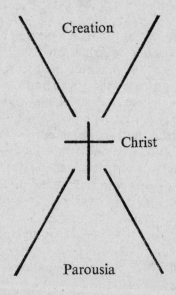

Creation

Christ

Parousia

One model by which to picture it would be of a double cone, open at both ends to the whole of creation. God made all things and saw that they were good—that is for communion with himself. But rebellion entered in and God chose Abraham, one chosen for the sake of all, that his redeeming work might be channelled to all through a chosen people.

The story of the Old Testament is the story of the refining of the chosen people to the faithful remnant and Messianic hope. Then there comes a moment when, in Jesus abandoned to the cross, all comes to a focus in the one Suffering Servant, the Messiah, the faithful Israel, the obedient Son, all focussed into that solitary figure.

The Christian Church is Israel, reconstituted by the work of Christ and by the gift of his Spirit, with a gospel to preach to 'all the world' until 'all things are summed up in Christ'. So the pattern is constant. God's plan is universal; his means is through the particular. God's technique is the calling of some for the sake of all, which comes to its fine focus point in the Christ.

But the counterpoint to the calling of the faithful, is the recurrent unfaithfulness of the called.

In Paul's letters to the church in Corinth we have the fullest surviving picture of the actual day to day life of a local Christian community. The paradox runs right through all that he has to say to them. On one side he is continually reproaching them for their failures to be what they are called to be. There are schisms and boastings among them. There is sexual disturbance and pagan spiritual pride. They are prone to secular litigation and financial irresponsibility. They do not appreciate the proper place of women in the Church and they behave disgracefully at the Christian love feast. On one side of the account, they could scarcely seem more reprobate.

But on the other side they are 'called to be Saints', sanctified in Jesus Christ. Their bodies are the Temple of God, which is why all sexual immorality is forbidden. The fullest reciprocity between men and women is implied in Christian marriage. Every neighbour is to be reckoned as one for whom Christ died. They participate fully in the body and blood of Christ and so become literally members of His body. In chapter 13 the nature of *agape*, the distinctively Christian word for love, is uniquely hymned and in chapter 15 a full life here and now is made possible by the resurrection of Jesus from the dead. The Church is a body of sanctified sinners, a body of sinning saints.

This paradox is resolved only in the paradox of Christ himself. It is by sharing in the dying and rising of Christ that the Church becomes itself. The paradox has a double application. On the one hand, to share in the life of Christ is to share in his rejection by men and his acceptance by God. Thus we know the fellowship of his sufferings and the power of his resurrection. At the same time, to be in Christ, is to put to death the 'old man', the unregenerate part of human nature which has no place in Christ. "For the love of Christ constraineth us: . . . one died for all, therefore all died; . . . wherefore if any man is in Christ he is a new creature." (2 Cor. 5:14, 7 R.V.). "You died and your life is hid with Christ in God. When Christ who is our life shall be manifested, then shall ye also be with him manifested in glory. Mortify therefore your members which are upon the earth . . ." (Col. 3:3-5 R.V.).

And so the Church lives in two 'ages' simultaneously. Partly we share in the victory and glory of Christ:

partly we live in the world which is passing away. The Church is those who are so incorporated into Christ by faith, which includes the sacraments for its effective fullness, that we thereby share his pattern of dying and rising. Both baptism and eucharist speak of that rhythm. The dying is a perpetual 'mortifying' of all which is not wholly obedient to the Father with the same obedience as is shown by the Son. This is true of the Church in all its senses, the individual Christian, the local congregation, the regional church, the totality of Christians at any point in history. Only with the passing away of this age into the fullness of Christ will the tension be resolved.

This attempt briefly to state the understanding of the Church which the New Testament has in relation to the Christ is attempted here only to give the background to the 'Shame and Glory of the Church'. At any given point in the history of the Church, as at any given point in an individual life, there is a contradiction between what we are called to be in Christ and what we are in practice. The contradiction is resolved by faith, that is by a final and utter trust that God, in Christ, can make what we are into what we ought to be.

Just as any individual at a particular moment may be more particularly conscious of one form of failure, so in different times and ages, the Church stands more evidently condemned.

In our generation, the Church acknowledges the judgment of God most clearly where it recognises that in a world becoming increasingly unified, a divided Church is a scandal and in a world sharply divided between the rich and the poor, the Church is too much found on the side of the rich.

The Ecumenical Movement of recent decades has

been primarily a movement of penitence for our divisions. It has not so far proved a very fruitful repentance. The Church of England has its special reasons for shame. When the Convocations narrowly rejected, on July 8th, 1969, the plan for union with the Methodist Church in England, it denied its profession of fifty years and more. At least since the Lambeth Conference of 1920, the Church of England had expressed the desire to unite with all other Christians who would join on a basis of apostolic faith and order. The Church of England has yet to show that it is credible as a Church and that it is more than an association of irreconcilable parties held together by rapidly dissolving custom. I am convinced that we shall rediscover our soul, but let us not underestimate the searching character of the judgment of God any more than we must underestimate the strength of his mercy.

The unity of the Church is essential to its fulfilment of God's design for it as fellowship. Christians will never know their true identity, never know who they are in the world, until more of these scandalous barriers to their mutual recognition are removed. But, by the same token, a divided Church can never express the universality of God's people in an increasingly unified global civilisation. The Ecumenical Movement has never been exclusively concerned with the reunion of the Churches. Historically it also had its origins in the missionary movement and the social conscience of Christians. And it is now even clearer that the unity and the renewal and the mission of the Church are inexplicably intertwined as different aspects of the same demand of the one living God. Is it possible to catch some kind of glimpse of God's overall purpose in our time? As I see it, it is really very simple and very exciting.

In the providence of God, mankind over countless centuries has been evolving new possibilities of living together. The achievements of science and technology have, for the first time, made possible a human community covering the whole globe. Whether, from that base, we have a mission towards the rest of the solar system, or even of this galaxy, is still a question too remote to be very urgent, but is has at least dawned. Meanwhile, man's freedom is, as always, a two-edged weapon. Powers of creation are always at the same time possibilities of destruction.

But into this awe-inspiring situation comes the remembrance of the incarnation of the Son of God. Already in the later pages of the New Testament are these vivid pictures of the tremendous claims of the Christ. I quote only one of them:

> "He is the image of the invisible God, the first-born of all creation; for in him all things were created in heaven and on earth, visible and invisible, whether thrones or dominions or principalities or authorities —all things were created through him and for him. He is before all things, and in him all things hold together. He is the head of the body, the church; he is the beginning, the first-born from the dead, that in everything he might be pre-eminent. For in him all the fullness of God was pleased to dwell. (Colossians 1:15–19. R.S.V.).

In order to prepare the Church as the Body of Christ for the time when it can be a genuinely Catholic Church, i.e. belonging to the whole of humanity and not just one part of it, God is having to strip us down to the real and universal essentials, loosening up our local characteristics in order that we may belong to all mankind.

This, I am certain, is why God is putting the Church in the Christian West through a particularly searching time, whilst he is at the same time creating a community of Christians in Africa and Asia which is both genuinely local and genuinely catholic. We in the wealthy, white, western world, have come to take for granted all kinds of associations between the Body of Christ and political and social power and privilege which have no necessary connection with the gospel at all. We have got to learn to count these things as rubbish in order to gain Christ. We shan't like it—but we shan't expect to. We have all, in our own individual Christian experience, been through phases where God has had to strip off a good many things we had taken for granted, in order to set us free for a new chapter of Christian obedience and effectiveness. In this way, the description of the Christian Church in the world, written many centuries ago in the *Shepherd of Hermas* becomes vividly real:

> "They dwell in their own country but only as sojourners; they bear their share in all things as citizens, and they endure all hardships as strangers. Every foreign country is a fatherland to them, and every fatherland is foreign . . . They obey the established laws, and they surpass the laws in their own lives . . . Their existence is on earth, but their citizenship is in heaven."

Seen positively like this, a lot of things which seemed only uncomfortable, become suddenly meaningful.

But it also means that we have to be a listening Church. When the Church exercised a good deal more secular power than it does now or is likely to in the future, we rather got into the habit of laying down the law and expecting people to listen or else—! Now they have largely stopped listening and they will not start again to listen until they have reason to believe that we, in our turn, have listened first so that we can speak what they really want to know.

And so 'let the world write the agenda'—for the local church.

By this I mean that we shall only really effectively discover how to fulfil our Lord's prayer: 'Thy name be hallowed, Thy Kingdom come, Thy Will be done on earth'—if we are not only deeply attentive to God himself through prayer and attending to his word in all the ways we have considered—and this comes first—but also by attending to the needs of our fellow men and women, the needs they feel and the needs they have yet to discover.

Take a simple example from the foreign mission field. When Christian missionaries from the West first arrived in far countries, they had to start by learning the language of the people they were working amongst, observing their customs and seeing where their real needs lay. Part of what we mean by rightly talking about England today as being a 'mission field' is that we too have to learn, almost literally, the language of those who do not understand our Christian phrases, to look carefully at the patterns of life which modern education and social conditions, the mass media and popular literature, are creating. It means that in our Parochial Church Councils and Church Groups, we should find ourselves seeking out the other people in our neighbourhood who also care about the welfare and happiness of our fellow human beings. For example, should we not invite some of the local doctors (if not already there) to come and tell us where they find the chief causes of unhappiness to lie. In some areas, we ought to take active steps to get into touch with the whole-time social workers, with their own high standards and training, to see what the Probation Officers, the Psychiatric Social Workers, the Welfare Officers and others can teach us about where the men and women around us are most in need.

The list could be a long one, but the main point is simple; if we are going to do a really effective missionary job we have got to know the language and the lives and the needs of ordinary men and women around us, who never come near us in our churches.

Social service is not a substitute for preaching the Gospel, but the Christian gospel is concerned with the whole man in his whole life, as we can see from studying the ministry of Jesus. But we have got to do a good deal more going out and looking and listening. It has been said that the Church structures which we have inherited are 'Come' structures—where they ought to be 'Go' structures—that is to say, we too easily think that we do our job by inviting other people to come where *we* are, instead of going out to find them where *they* are. "The Church lives by mission as a fire lives by burning."

If God's big designs really come home to the little local church in such ways as these, that gives us something indeed to do and something to pray about.

FOR THE CHURCH

O God, rouse thy Church, lest we sleep and miss men's need of thee and thy yearning love for men.

O God, cleanse thy Church and forgive our lack of zeal for thy Kingdom.

O God, set thy Church ablaze with the fire of thy Spirit, that we may spend and be spent for thy gospel, thy will and thy glory through all our days.

FAITH IN GOD'S WORKING

O God, who has created the universe and art ever at work in it to restore the harmony broken by the self-will of men: Give us quiet, confident, joyful faith in thee, that our eyes may ever look in expectation to thy love and power, rather than to the power of evil or to the weakness of men.

Help us to stand firm in the assurance that thou art at work in all that happens, in the foolishness and rebellion of men as well as in their efforts for goodness, turning all to thy loving purpose. Fill us with joy and hope in believing, through him who was victorious over sin, enmity, defeat and death, even Jesus Christ, our beloved Lord.[5]

[5] George Appleton, from *One Man's Prayers*.

Behaviour

O England! full of sinne, but most of sloth;
Spit out thy flegme, and fill thy brest with glorie.

George Herbert, *The Temple*

When I spoke to a journalist about the lectures which lie behind this book I mentioned, among many other things, that the talk about behaviour would refer to the question which is being raised today as to whether there are any rules which are absolutely binding. For instance, the commandment 'Thou shalt not commit adultery' is held by some not to be so absolute that there might be circumstances when to break it was less wrong than to keep it. Knowing the habits of newspapers, I was not surprised to see the prominent headline 'Bishop to talk on adultery—when it might not be wrong'. Needless to say, the article under the headline was not nearly so unbalanced. And I did not expect to see an equally prominent headline 'Bishop says adultery is always wrong'. That would not be news. But this little incident reveals two facts about the contemporary situation which may serve as our starting point—that all moral questions, especially sexual ones, are publicly discussed in sensational terms and that, behind the sensationalism, there lies a widespread, radical questioning of inherited attitudes.

Let us look first at the sensationalism. The effect of the mass media on modern sensitivity is one of the biggest moral questions of our time. What has been happening to us? For centuries the great mass of mankind had their minds formed primarily by the handing down of inherited attitudes through the family and the intimate circle. Mothers were—and still are—the *primary* teachers. To their home-teaching was added the store of legend and song which circulated around the fireside, the village inn and village green and the tales of the returned traveller or the talk of the wandering teacher. Slowly, writing evolved to record remembered knowledge; only a tiny minority could read or write—and they became the centres from which unfamiliar ideas radiated. Rumour and exaggeration have always flourished, but the circle they influenced was limited—though the wildness of the old folk-tales could outshine the most sensational Sunday papers' headlines. But everyone knew they were wild stories and genuinely *new* ideas had to gain currency by word of mouth and be tested by the experience of those who heard them. It was in such a setting that Jesus taught—by word of mouth, to groups no larger than can hear one man, who repeated to others what they had heard. But the definition of a 'civilised world' was one where speech could be captured and conveyed by writing—and the Graeco-Roman world was, in that sense, a civilised one. For another fifteen centuries, Europe was a world in which the mass could only listen. The few who could read and write had a monopoly over what could be *widely* spread.

Then came printing. In Europe, its discovery coincided with the Renaissance and the Reformation. For the first time it was possible to reproduce in hundreds and thousands what had been single precious manuscripts; for the first time there was some point for the average man in being able to read. New ideas could spread as never before and the new ideas of the Reformers exploded upon Europe, especially through their appeal to the Bible, which it was now possible for the first time for any large number of people actually to read.

We live in the next big explosion, that of the electronic age in which, by an odd irony, just as more people are literate than ever before there is a diminishing need to be so, as radio and television tell you the modern version of the old tales heard on the village green. We all live increasingly in the 'global village'. So the old crudities, the rumours, the exaggerations, the sensational gossip are available to millions simultaneously.

The relevance of all this to our theme of 'behaviour' is that any challenge to accepted standards, any startling item, any crude over-simplifying of complex issues has an opportunity as never before to become common property overnight. The detailed argument, the subtle analysis, the balanced judgment—all still go on—but they were always the concern of a minority and of the minority who, until very recently, had a virtual monopoly of the means of communication. Even the 'popular press' of the last two generations was only 'popular' to those who could read. The age of electronic communication knows no such barriers—and today the radio loudspeaker blares in the bazaars of Calcutta; transistor sets pour out from Japan all over the Afro-Asian world; T.V. sets are among the commonest consumer-goods in the U.S.S.R.

We are confronted by the double phenomenon

(a) that new ideas, moulding behaviour, can spread as never before.

(b) that the media through which they travel have a

built-in preference for over-simplifying precisely because they are genuinely *popular*.

So any discussion of *behaviour* today must reckon with these possibilities for changing it on a wholly new scale.

It is on this background of instantaneous and simplified communication that we need to see the beleaguered state of Christian morality. For there is no doubt that Christian morality is on trial. Of course, in one sense, it always has been—in the sense that G. K. Chesterton meant when he wrote "It is not that Christianity has been tried and found wanting: it has been found difficult and not tried". There have always been those who have failed to practise the Christian ethic, as they understood it, though there has been a variety of ways of accounting for the failure. The least pleasant way is hypocrisy—'the tribute which vice pays to virtue'. More wholesome is the good-natured admission that virtue is really too difficult and really not such fun — as in the Wife of Bath in *The Canterbury Tales* and Falstaff and their whole rollicking crew—lovable creatures —and more so when they admit, in soberer moments, that they would like to get around to being good some day. But what the hypocrite and the roisterer have in common, with many shades between, is the admission that the Christian code is *true*, whatever reasons they give for not keeping it.

What is newer amongst us is the wide range of those who deny that it is true, that the Christian standard is one that ought to be attempted. I say 'amongst us' because I am not here thinking of the ethics which spring from the great non-Christian religious. It would be an interesting study to compare the codes of behaviour which stem from Islam, Hinduism, Buddhism—but beyond my competence and outside our immediate concern. Yet I believe it has this relevance, that part of the agnosticism about ethics today derives from a vague but widespread awareness that anthropology and comparative religion have revealed considerable differences in socially acceptable conduct. One is hard put to it to name any moral injunction which is *universally* acceptable. You can literally get away with murder where the blood-feud is part of the social pattern—and theft can be a virtue when the next tribe's cattle is at stake. And anyway—how does war differ from a sophisticated blood-feud or imperial colonisation of the black man's land differ from old-style cattle-raiding? Part of our confusion arises from knowing more than our fathers did about how the other half lives—and the question mark it puts against our own assumptions.

But quite apart from this new relativism, the doubt whether there are any universal rules, there is the challenge of those who believe that the Christian rules are wrong—or even that where they are right, they are held for the wrong reasons. A 'humanist', I suppose, might be defined as one who believes that ethical standards can be honoured without seeking any authority for them in the transcendent, whether the 'transcendent' is another name for Almighty God or only for the absolute moral law of the non-Christian deist. There is no need to plead for the personal sincerity and integrity of such people. You can not engage today in any work for peace or racial equality or prison reform without finding yourself working alongside them. And millions of people whose social consciences never move them far from their own T.V. sets have witnessed the passion of Bertrand

Russell, the courtesy of A. J. Ayer, the sincerity of Ritchie Calder.

But for the Christian, they are not always acceptable allies. The issues come up thick and fast on which Christian traditions are challenged. In my time as a member of the House of Lords, matters have moved from academic discussion to actual legislation touching upon capital punishment, homosexual offences, divorce, contraceptive advice for the unmarried, abortion and euthanasia.

I need only to give that list to reveal the third factor in our beleaguered state—in addition to the relativism that comes from awareness of other cultures and the challenge of positive humanism, there is the uncertainty within the Christian camp itself. Are such the fifth column who are betraying the besieged city—or are they the intrepid scouts surveying the land we should sally forth to conquer? Not one of the political issues I mentioned finds us Christians undivided. I have been challenged for supporting the abolition of capital punishment on the ground that it was a scriptural injunction: how far homosexual conduct is always a sin, let alone a crime, is questioned by some Christian writers; divorce brings us back to the headline I started with! Those Christians who hold that *all* marriages are of their nature indissoluble are bound to regard as the endorsement of adultery the attitude of those other Christians who accept 're-marriage' after divorce as the best solution to a tragic situation: contraception within marriage is notoriously splitting the mind of Christendom whilst the choice—if it is a choice—between contraceptive advice for the unmarried or more abortion or more unwanted and illegitimate babies is one you can't duck if you work amongst the young: euthanasia raises the same issue of what responsibility the Church—or at any rate the individual Christian citizen—has for those whose lack of faith prevents them from accepting the Christian answer.

The situation has been further clouded lately by the reassertion (for it is no new claim) that there are no fixed rules of Christian behaviour at all, but only 'situational ethics' i.e. the response of the individual Christian in the spirit of Christ-like love to the immediate situation in which he finds himself. Even so conservative a writer as Bishop K. E. Kirk maintained that nothing can be said to be 'wrong in itself'—or at least it can only be a principle you may assert once. For if it is asserted of two or more principles, there is always the possibility that two such principles may be found in conflict with each other—then one or other must yield and then the principle itself is demonstrated as false.[1]

But this reluctance to say that there are *any* actions which are *always* wrong, attracted much alarmed attention at the time of the publication of the British Council of Churches pamphlet on *Sex and Morality* and, about the same time, another pamphlet called *Towards a Quaker view of Sex*. The reaction was one of alarm because many felt that this was to leave the door wide open for people—especially young people—to argue that the *generally* wrong thing was the thing they wanted at the moment to do and therefore, for them in their situation, it was all right. Even Bishop Kirk admitted that to refuse to say that anything was always wrong in itself, although logically necessary, was to make it more difficult to know how to teach the young. He concluded that all we could do was firmly to say that theft or lying are

[1] See his *Threshold of Ethics*, p. 30.

wrong—and leave the discovery of the necessary qualifications to a more mature stage of development.

Certainly there is a way of presenting 'situational ethics' which is to treat altogether irresponsibly the accumulated experience of mankind. But one mature mind which I greatly admired[2] writing in *Soundings* distinguished beween what existentialists call 'authentic' and 'un-authentic' ways of living and concluded 'the basic misconduct is to live without sincerity and integrity'. If there is *one* thing which is *always* wrong, that seems to me a good way of describing it, and in no danger of coming into conflict with another principle which is more true.

I do not think there is any need to labour the point any further; behaviour is an area in which there are not only a lot of people who have questions to put to Christians, but an area in which Christians put a good many questions to each other—and so to God. Can we take a fresh look at what he seems to answer?

It would be nice to feel that we had either a book of rules which left no loose ends or the assurance that there are no loose ends because there are no rules. To say "it would be nice to feel" is really to talk about conscience, for in either of these solutions, conscience would still raise its voice. It is conscience which would send us to look up the book of rules (if there was one) and conscience which would be relieved to know that it is all right to go ahead (if there was not). No discussion of right behaviour, in other words, can ignore 'conscience'. What then is it?

The best definition I know is the one given by the

---

[2] G. F. Woods, one of my examining chaplains, whose early death was a grave loss to clear theology.

late Dr. K. E. Kirk,[3] that it is 'the mind of man making moral judgments'. Such a definition brings conscience out of the mists of metaphysics into daily life, where it operates. We are well aware of ourselves making other judgments—aesthetic judgments about buildings or music or pictures; personal judgments about the character, reliability and so forth of others. This illuminates the way conscience operates like such other judgments, it is a function of our rational personality, making allowance for known prejudices, aware of gaps in the data, acknowledging the need to be instructed by the accumulated wisdom of the past and the insights of the present and then—when nothing more can be collected that appears to be relevant, making the decision and acting on it. Conscience, like all other judgment-making, is thus both limited and absolute. We know perfectly well that we may be mistaken, as we may be when choosing a new L.P. record or a business partner. But we also know that there comes a point at which we must decide—and that's that. There is no further court of appeal—we must accept responsibility. (For of course the decision to let someone else decide is still just as unescapably *our* decision as any other—it may be cowardice or it may be simply the wise admission that, at least in this instance, that other may know best.)

Would 'conscience' be fully satisfied if there were a book with all the rules? Many men have thought so. Part of our heritage as Christians is Judaism and much of the Old Testament is precisely such a book of rules. It all sprang from a lively awareness that God is a God of righteousness and demands righteousness from his children. At the heart of the rules stand the Ten Commandments and their authority for Christians we must

[3] *The Threshold of Ethics*, Chapter 1.

consider soon. But Judaism contained much more than the Decalogue. It is an elementary point in Old Testament literary criticism that much of the earlier material was worked over and edited by a school of priestly editors, who were concerned to bring the whole of life within the Law of God and relate it to worship. The Pentateuch (the first five books of the Old Testament) reflects their activity, especially evident in such a book as Leviticus where, you will remember, are detailed regulations covering the whole of daily life—birth, marriage, agriculture and the treatment of animals, land tenure, labour relations and much else. But, detailed as it was, it was not enough. On top of that comes the Talmud, the rabbinic commentary which elaborates more and more to fill in the missing details. The New Testament is full of reflections upon the rabbinic commentary, such as the ruling that to pluck ears of corn on the Sabbath and roll it in your hands to release the grain counts as the prohibited labour of grinding on the Sabbath. Jesus' quarrel with such an approach only continues a criticism which already appears within the Old Testament itself, that of the prophets.

For one of the difficulties about the 'book of rules' solution is 'Who can you trust to write it?' Men being men, there is an inherent tendency for those who elaborate the rules to develop a vested interest in what they write, to slant it to their own advantage. Again and again the Old Testament prophets burst into flame in protest against those who have prostituted the rules to make them serve their own interest.

But there is a deeper objection to rules as the sufficient answer. The more detailed the rules become the less living-space they allow for spontaneity, for the endless variety and richness of human living, for the unforeseen, the uniquely personal qualities of love, compassion, generosity. If you really try to work to rule, you end up with something much smaller than life. Sooner or later you come up against something which the rules do not fit and, if you are to live, then the rules must be blown sky-high. And where is conscience then?

So we swing to the other extreme and see how conscience manages without any rules. Let life be lived completely in the spontaneity of personal relationships as the only guide. Yet that is soon to run conscience into difficulties of another kind. If my unfettered conscience is to make every decision existentially in the moment of choice, how am I to be guarded against making all decisions into decisions of self-interest? Obviously by seeking to see the other person as one with a right to the freedoms I desire for myself—and so we come to such a 'golden rule' as "Do unto others as you would they should do unto you". But how much does that solve? In practice it is often as hard to know what I would that others should do to me as to know what I should do to them. When my interests and their interests clash, is there any place outside both of us to which we can look for some kind of objective standard against which both our interests are to be measured? If we then have recourse to some criterion of general social good, we are not only dangerously near to being back with some kind of rules again, but we are also still without any guide if the social good by which we measure personal good is itself in conflict with another social good, the rights of some other society as it comes into conflict with our society. And how can my conscience adjudicate in that situation without setting up to be something a good deal more than I can claim for my conscience. 'My' conscience only has validity at that point if I can believe that it owes an obligation to something, or someone, who has the right to authority over all consciences. And that right constitutes the point of reference into something which can only be described as a law-giver. Which is where we came in when we tried to get out.

At this point, let us remember that we are Christians —or at least asking what the Christian religion has to say about the grounds of behaviour.

People sometimes refer—I remember especially hearing the phrase in the rather old-fashioned kind of idealist Trade Unionism or W.E.A. class—to 'the simple teaching of Jesus'. If only it were! But 'simple' seems to me the last word to apply to something like the Sermon on the Mount, at least if by 'simple' you mean something of which the meaning is perfectly clear so that you know exactly what you are expected to do.

Listen again to some of this 'simple teaching' (Matt. 5–6; N.E.B.). " 'How blest are those who know their need of God; the kingdom of Heaven is theirs. How blest are the sorrowful; they shall find consolation. How blest are those of a gentle spirit; they shall have the earth for their possession. How blest are those who hunger and thirst to see right prevail; they shall be satisfied. How blest are those who show mercy; mercy shall be shown to them. How blest are those whose hearts are pure; they shall see God. How blest are the peacemakers; God shall call them his sons. How blest are those who have suffered persecution for the cause of right; the kingdom of Heaven is theirs.' " (vv. 3–10.)

" 'You have learned that our forefathers were told, "Do not commit murder; anyone who commits murder must be brought to judgment." But what I tell you is this: Anyone who nurses anger against his brother must be brought to judgment. If he abuses his brother he must answer for it to the court; if he sneers at him he will have to answer for it in the fires of hell.'" (vv. 21–22.)

"'You have learned that they were told, "Do not commit adultery." But what I tell you is this: If a man looks on a woman with a lustful eye, he has already committed adultery with her in his heart.'" (vv. 27–28.)

"'You have learned that they were told, "Eye for eye, tooth for tooth." But what I tell you is this: Do not set yourself against the man who wrongs you. If someone slaps you on the right cheek, turn and offer him your left.'" (vv. 38–39.)

"'There must be no limit to your goodness,' as your heavenly Father's goodness knows no bounds.'" (v. 48.)

"Be ye therefore perfect"—in the more familiar version "as your Father in heaven is perfect"! Simple indeed—it's downright impossible. It's true that there is much in the teaching of Jesus which provides heart-warming ideals for us to try, not too despairingly, to follow—the parables of the prodigal son, for example, or the good Samaritan. The world would obviously be a happier place if more people behaved like that—whereas if we carried out the Sermon on the Mount, organised society as we know it would simply collapse.

And there is much else which is manifestly unfair—e.g. Matthew 20:1–16, the parable of the Labourers in the Vineyard. Where would society be if the lazy were paid as much as the industrious? Many people already complain that unemployment rates are dangerously near to the minimum wage.

I may seem to be guying the teaching of Jesus. God

forbid—but what I do want to bring home is that the teaching of Jesus is totally misunderstood if we think of it only as a set of moral injunctions which we simply have to carry out. A revised version, in fact, of the old book of rules. If we think of it like that, it simply reduces us to despair.

Or perhaps it would be truer to say that it is good that we *should* think of it like that in order that we may be reduced to despair and so compelled to look at it again to see what it really is.

The teaching of Jesus is not a set of moral precepts which we are expected simply to go out and put into practice. It is rather a factual description of what life is like in the kingdom of God. The beatitudes are not advice—they are statements of fact, of how things *are* in God's sight. Again and again, Jesus begins his teaching "The Kingdom of God is *like* . . ." and then goes on to describe—the merchantman seeking goodly pearls, the farmer who finds a treasure hid in a field, the net cast into the sea, the city set on a hill, the bridegroom who comes unexpectedly, the lord of the manor who leaves his stewards in charge—and a host of other pictures.

In other words, the ethical teaching of Jesus is first and last a claim upon *allegiance*. It is a declaration of what God is like and a call to come into his sphere of rule, his 'kingdom', where response to him has this distinctive quality about it. Now this is not quite like either of the other two ways we have been thinking about, yet it has bearings upon both of them. It is not simply a new set of 'rules', but it does refer to a 'rule', the reign or kingdom of God. The kind of conduct which follows is not without content, because its content is wholly dependent upon the character of God, so that

Jesus can sum it all up by saying "You must therefore be all goodness, just as your heavenly Father is all good". Neither, though, is it an invitation to unlimited spontaneity. It is true that it goes beneath external rules to the springs of behaviour in motive. But it transcends the rules not by ignoring them but by going beyond them.

"Do not suppose that I have come to abolish the law and the prophets; I did not come to abolish but to complete." (Matt. 5 : 17; N.E.B.)

Looking back then to the two strands as we saw them in the Old Testament, the Priestly laws and the Prophetic protest against them, we see Jesus claiming to fulfil, to complete, them both. *The Law still stands* in the sense that Jesus calls us into obedience to a God whose love has a *content*. Because he is the Creator-God, the world he has made has a shape, it has laws, rules, structures, which we can only harm ourselves by ignoring. The Decalogue still stands at the back of Christian ethics as the reminder that God makes rules which cannot be ignored without disaster. *The Prophets still stand* in that these laws can never be tidied up into a fool-proof, all-embracing code which leaves no room for spontaneity, generosity, compassion and the unpredictable uniqueness of every separate confrontation with the Living God in his creatures. In this sense, Christian ethics are always 'situational ethics' in being response to the living Father. But they are not 'situational' in the sense that they have no consistency—for their content is always governed by the consistency of the character of God. "I, the Lord, change not, therefore ye, O sons of Jacob, are not consumed." (Malachi 3 : 6; R.V.)

What, then, is Christian behaviour? How does Christianity show?

If obedience to God the Creator involves, as it were, working with the grain of the universe, finding out what is inevitable and co-operating with it, then there will be large areas in which Christian morality is not distinctive. We accept this in all other areas of life—so why not in moral conduct too. There is no specifically Christian bridge-building or astronomy or cooking—only good and bad bridge-building and astronomy and cooking. It is significant that we use 'good and bad' (ethical words) to describe these non-ethical standards, meaning 'what works'. How far is 'good conduct' simply 'behaviour that works'—i.e. is evidently successful. But successful in what? Here Christian and e.g. humanist may begin to disagree and we shall come to that in a minute. But let us recognise that Christian behaviour over vast ranges of human living will not differ *visibly* from non-Christian.

Secondly, there is obviously a range of Christian behaviour which is peculiar—all that pertains to 'church-going'. It is an area in which we are a little uneasy today.

"The most conspicuous and clear-cut way in which it shows is that the Christian has a whole range of extra duties, prayer and church-going and financial support of his Church, which the sceptic does not merely omit but feels absolutely no obligation to perform and perhaps a clear obligation not to perform. Whatever other moral differences Christian or sceptic may want to insist upon, here is one significant distinction which both will want to make.

"The Christian, like his fellow-citizens, is aware of duties to other people, but on top of these he is mindful

of a duty to God which his sceptical friends do not
share.

"But how, it needs to be insistently asked, is one to
be sure in a given case which claim is God's claim? To
identify it flatly with the specifically 'religious' duty and
let one's other duties take care of themselves is re-
ligiosity, not holiness. In easy cases this will be obvious.
A reasonable Christian is not likely to leave a sheep in
a pit on the Sabbath day. He will look on feeding the
hungry as a higher priority than putting flowers in his
parish church, at least if the question is presented plainly
to him. He is rather less inclined to sit and read the Bible
while his wife washes up than to sit and read the Sunday
papers when he ought to be in Church.

"But the problem is not always so clear-cut. Are
churches never to be made beautiful as long as there are
hungry people in the world? Are the hungry ever to be
converted, or only to be fed? At what point then should
spiritual need assume priority over material need? And
how is one to compare one's own spiritual need with the
material need of another? Can one serve God better by
going to Communion or by taking charge of an ex-
hausted mother's children so that she can have a long
sleep?" [4]

The uneasy conscience of clergy and laity alike will
only be healed when *together* we reassess 'church-
going' as being, like every other aspect of Chrisian behaviour, meaningful only as part of the response of love
to the being of God, in which 'duty' is not ignored but
exceeded in the glad *giving* of what we want to give
because of a relationship which is already there.

There is no denying that the tradition of Christian

[4] Helen Oppenheimer, *The Character of Christian Morality*
(Faith Press, 1965).

behaviour is most confident and clear-cut in the realm of personal relationships. This is surprising when we remember the debt of Christianity to Judaism not only with its immense emphasis on ritual law (Sabbath-keeping, kosher meat, etc.) but also the elaboration of its social code. But it is not surprising in light of the Incarnation—the unique feature of the Christian religion. Here is God living a human life and so transforming our conception of its possibilities and implications. From this springs the uniqueness of the Christian teaching on sex, marriage and the family. Life-long monogamy gets a certain support from the natural law—i.e. the area common to all men because it works —in the recognition of the long-term dependence of human offspring upon the emotional security which only two reliable parents can give. So far, most people would agree, is our ideal. But to speak of the union of man and wife as comparable to the union between Christ and his Church is to introduce an altogether new dimension of utter mutual commitment, of living in and for the other which goes far deeper and higher.

The case against fornication is powerful for those who have any appreciation of the complexity of sexual relations. Humanists who run Brook clinics are well aware of the sheer misery, frustration and self-destruction which young people bring on themselves by supposing that the only purpose of sex is 'fun', i.e. short term pleasure, or that sexual 'appetite' is strictly analogous to the desire for a meal or a drink. All sexual relations, and, supremely, full intercourse, are between complex persons who need and seek enduring commitment at all levels of being. What is wrong with extra-marital coitus is not what is given but what is withheld. But Dr. Alex Comfort, as a sensitive humanist, seems

to me to be saying all this when he lays down the rule
for personal relationships that one should always desire
for the other their true good in all aspects of their personality. Again, all this is taken into new dimensions
when St. Paul says: "Do you not know that your bodies
are limbs and organs of Christ. Shall I then take from
Christ his bodily parts and make them over to a har-
lot? . . . You do not belong to yourselves; you were
bought at a price. Then honour God in your body."
(I Cor. 6:15, 20; N.E.B.)

Future co-operation with our fellows in solving
human problems must surely lie in this combination of
seeking common ground with other analysts of human
nature, rooted for us as Christians in our interpretation
of the work of God as Creator, together with the deeper
insights into human nature and its destiny which we find
in the Incarnate Son of God and his redemption of men
for eternal life. It is already clear that this does not
provide easy or conclusive solutions over matters like
contraception, abortion or euthanasia. But tell me of
any big problem to which there are easy or conclusive
answers. The difficulties do not seem to be other than
those which belong to our finitude.

We must not forget that whole range of questions
which are more often thought of as social or political
rather than personal. (It is an unreal distinction for
I have just referred to personal questions to which
we are having to give social and political answers,
whilst every social and political action is finally dependent upon an aggregate of personal attitudes. But
the distinction is commonly made.) As Archbishop Wil-
liam Temple pointed out [5] the assumption that Christianity has nothing to say to social and political affairs

[5] *Christianity and Social Order*, 1942.

is a very recent one, and would have been meaningless to earlier centuries. Part of the reproach of the young generation who went on protest marches, as boys and girls emerged from their shared sleeping-bags, was that the older generation, which was very dogmatic about sex, lapsed into confused silence about war.

W. H. Thorpe, (writing as a Christian as well as a biologist in *Science, Man and Morals*) speaks of "the two supreme problems of our day—the population explosion and the role of nuclear energy" as being soluble only if mankind takes the direction of 'involution' or 'convergent integration'—that is "instead of fanning-out into new environments and to form new lines, which is the characteristic pattern of animal evolution and of human racial differentiation so far, the only and inevitable course open to the faces and cultures of man in the future is to become more and more unified: to come to express in fact the supreme ideal of diversity within unity". [6]

"Human evolution is biology plus culture." But why I quote this particular passage is that he cites in support of it J. B. S. Haldane, Karl Polanyi, Teilhard de Chardin and the later Epistles of St. Paul. In other words, at this level of ethical problem too, approach must be that of the patient search for common ground with all competent and sincere workers for truth and happiness *plus* the appeal to God known in Christ as the source of new dimensions of understanding.

Two final points.

First, the appeal to God in Christ may, at any moment, lead not to complementing what is affirmed by non-Christians but to contradicting it. This follows *theologically* from remembering that although this is the

[6] Op. cit., pp. 153–4.

world which God made, it is also the world which
crucified Jesus. It follows *sociologically* because two
groups may develop different power-interests from different ideologies. The Nazi death-camps for the Jews
are an ugly reminder that the undeniable compassion
which lies behind the current plea for euthanasia might
be swallowed up in ugly causes—and to remember that
must be one factor in assessing its claims. So far in this
country the deep roots in Christian faith of our social
and political institutions have prevented any costly clash
between Christian conscience and the political will. But
the rumblings that accompany the discussion—and the
legislation—about divorce, abortion and euthanasia
may indicate the piling up of a storm which will some
day break.

Lastly, I end where I began, with the nature of
modern communications. The fact that in our 'global village', in our one world in which millions live on top of
each other, with instantaneous communications developed far ahead of any common mind or even a single
universe of discourse, in such a world, much thinking will
be done in slogans and facile emotions find quick expression. 'Ho Ho Ho Chi Min', 'Long live Chairman Mao',
'Uhuru', 'Harambee', 'Yanks—or British—go home'.
The age-old device of the battlecry now has a resonance
far wider than its own battle-field—or even its own
cricket-ground. In such a world the delicate task of
restating old duties for fresh occasions, and of discern-
ing new duties for occasions which have never before
arisen, is fraught with frightening difficulties. To speak
at all is to risk being misrepresented through a mega-
phone; not to speak may be the literally unspeakable
betrayal. Yet all the while, the stakes invested in human
misery or glory mount higher. We who are called the

Body of Christ are for that same reason called to an identification with the world, in its misery and its glory, which will be more eloquent than anything we say. There are times when we must say things: when we do, let us try not to add to the slogans which rouse emotion without clarifying thought. Yet we must not be silent for fear of being misquoted. Beneath the strident voices, mankind seeks its peace. We Christians have met one who said with a breath-taking authority "My peace I give unto you". Our concern with ethics is a compassionate concern that others—as well as ourselves—may find peace. It will not be found through acquiescence in false estimates of what men and women are *really* like, for that would be only to land them in the misery which follows from mistaking our own true nature. Behaviour is only *right* behaviour if it makes us into the kind of creature which we truly are, those who have been made in the image of God and are restored from our damaged image to know God and enjoy him for ever.

The Last Word

Love bade me welcome: yet my soul drew back,
Guiltie of dust and sinne ...
You must sit down, sayes Love, and taste my meat:
So I did sit and eat.

George Herbert, *The Temple*

God always has the last word. That is what is so intolerable about him. You can't win. But if you want to win, you shouldn't tangle with God.

God has the Last Word over Religion

So it is rather a joke to write books about him. As if they could ever say anything true. But since he does have the last word, what is the use of having a mind at all if you do not use it to try to understand God. We *must* try to express him, for there is nothing else worth trying to express in the last resort. Everything starts from him, lives in him, ends in him—if he is there at all. Not that he always claims direct attention. Most of the time he does not. Because what he makes is good, to pay attention to what he makes is also good. That is what all poetry and drama are doing. That is the meaning of every artist—that he should discern reality and express it. That is to share in creation—taking what is given and interpreting it. Only God can interpret non-being. Creation *ex nihilo* is God's copyright.

So God has the last word in art. Even to deny that is

to invite that disconcerting whisper—for it is rarely his custom to shout.

> "Just when you are safest, there's a sunset touch
>   A fancy from a flower-bell, someone's death,
>   A chorus ending from Euripides—
>   And that's enough for fifty hopes and fears
>   As old and new at once as nature's self
>   To rap and knock and enter in our soul,
>   Take hands and dance there, a fantastic ring,
>   Around the ancient idol on his base again—
>   The grand Perhaps! We look on helplessly.
>   There the old misgivings, crooked questions are—
>   This good God—what he could do if he would,
>   Would if he could—then must have done long
>   since;
>   If so, when, where and how? Some way must be—
>   Once feel about, and soon or late you hit
>   Some sense, in which it might be, after all,
>   Why not, 'The Way, the Truth, the Life' [1]

In the beginning was the Word, as well as in the end. And when it was made flesh, he was full of grace and truth. That is why all art and science are in danger of being exploded by finding him. But their danger is as nothing compared with the danger to religion. The peril to the artist is nothing compared with the peril to the preacher. For the preacher is always in danger of standing outside his own message, of supposing that you can talk about God without talking to him. To talk about God without getting involved in him is what Kierkegaard meant by the 'professor of theology'. "Professor— of what? Why, of the fact that Christ was crucified and

[1] Robert Browning, *Bishop Blougram's Apology*.

the Apostles scourged . . . of the fact that another person
was put to death." The 'professor' is the one who
describes, instead of following, Christ and his Apostles.
This is the peril of being religious—that religion becomes a substitute for God.

Jesus, the first word and the last word, is forever
bursting through religion and irreligion alike. Suppose
you have him under control—and 'he passed through
the midst of them and went his way'. That is why no
theological formula, no liturgical embalming, no institutional embodiment can be allowed the last word. But
then neither may any denial. Atheism is no safer than
theism. Over both, God retains the last word.

God has the Last Word over Death

"This Jesus, whom ye slew, God raised." God had
the last word then—and he keeps it. It speaks eloquently
of human nature that when goodness was uniquely embodied, we killed him. God spoke more eloquently
when he refused to accept that killing as final.

The crucifixion may condemn us, but it does not
embarrass us. We can understand the crucifixion: it
happened in public in broad daylight. The resurrection
embarrasses us. It happened secretly in the dark. It is
so blatantly a miracle: and miracles are by definition
embarrassing. And yet—what is the significance of the
crucifixion apart from the resurrection? If Christ had
not been raised, his death would not be remembered,
except in prose anthologies, like Plato's remembrance
of the death of Socrates in the *Phaedo*. Because a hand-
ful of men and women soon became convinced that
Jesus lives (in some sense different from that in which
Socrates 'lives') the cross is remembered. If there were
no Easter, there would be no cause to 'call that Friday

Good'. The Church is the community which lives by remembering Jesus—but it would not remember him at all if he were only dead. So—a particular death sets all death into a new perspective. As St. Paul puts it, "if Christ has not been raised, then our preaching is in vain and your faith is in vain". (I Cor. 15:14; R.S.V.)

Death, apart from Christ, is both a friend and an enemy, but more of an enemy than a friend. Death, in nature, is a friend who removes what is finished with. Just as the new leaves can not appear except the old ones be pushed off, so death continually clears the way for renewal. But man transcends nature in his reluctance ever to be finished with: to *be* human is to make some protest about the finality of death. Man is the only animal which buries its dead with symbols of protest.

Death, in Christ, is both an enemy and a friend, but more of a friend than an enemy. Death is the last enemy because death is the final demonstration of futility. Just when every activity of the human spirit, in art, in politics, in love, is on the point of proclaiming its self-sufficiency, death gives it the lie. So the real question is 'Can you believe in a life before death?' In Christ, we are offered not immortality but resurrection to life eternal. The promise in Christ is such communion with God here that it can not be broken hereafter. Then death becomes more of a friend than an enemy. "For me to live is Christ, and to die is gain . . . I am hard pressed between the two. My desire is to depart and be with Christ, for that is far better." But—St. Paul continued—(Phil. 1:21–25; R.S.V.) so long as you need me around the place, I am content to stay.

'Survival after death' seems to me neither here nor there and of no great consequence to the Christian. It is true that the elaborately collected evidence of survival makes the old-fashioned materialism—'We snuff out like a candle'—look rather silly. But that, surely, looks rather silly anyway; the neat divisions between body, mind and spirit are being called into question. Life appears to consist of varied manifestations of energy. I find nothing surprising in the thought that there is a hitherto unsuspected continuity between sensory and extra-sensory perception, between normal and paranormal psychology, between psychic energy before and after death. I am struck by the evidence that minds can be as trivial and as self-centred after death as before it— and by the apparent lack of communication from those who, before they died, had the deepest and the sweetest intimations of God and his glory. It may be that here is the material for a more satisfying re-statement of all the speculations which once produced Purgatory. Certainly I expect pretty radical treatment of some kind before my silly and trivial mind can contemplate God without pain. But I am content to wait to discover what kind of treatment.

Meanwhile, all the meagre resources of human language have been ransacked to try to imagine what that communion with God, which I now see only in puzzling reflections in a mirror, will be like face to face. Listen briefly to two who now know. C. S. Lewis tried to describe some of 'The Weight of Glory':

"When all the suns and nebulae have passed away, each one of you will still be alive. Nature is only the image, the symbol; but it is the symbol Scripture invites me to use. We are summoned to pass in through Nature, beyond her, into that splendour which she fitfully reflects.

And in there, in beyond Nature, we shall eat of the tree of life. At present, if we are reborn in Christ, the spirit in us lives directly on God; but the mind, and still more the body, receives life from Him at a thousand removes—through our ancestors, through our food, through the elements. The faint, far-off results of those energies which God's creative rapture implanted in matter when He made the worlds are what we now call physical pleasures; and even thus filtered, they are too much for our present management. What would it be to taste at the fountain-head that stream of which even these lower reaches prove so intoxicating? Yet that, I believe, is what lies before us. The whole man is to drink joy from the fountain of joy."[2]

Austin Farrer cried "Lord, I believe . . . in the Resurrection of the Body and the Life Everlasting".

"O my God, 'eye hath not seen, ear hath not heard, neither hath there entered into the heart of man' the provision that you have made for the happiness of your lovers. And yet, as the same scripture declares, you have revealed your bounty to us, for you have given us your Spirit to teach us what it bestows on us. And so by nature these things are not known, and yet by your Spirit they are most surely known; and our state is balanced between this sure knowledge and this blank ignorance. We are utterly ignorant of the conditions of that life: how our hands will be occupied, if we have hands; how we shall perceive, whether through five senses, or fifteen, or one. And since we have no knowledge of these most elementary things and could not understand the truth of them if it were told us, it seems doubly vain to enquire into deeper matters.

"Nevertheless it is these deeper matters that you,

[2] Reprinted in C. S. Lewis, *They Asked for a Paper* (Bles, 1962).

by your Spirit have made most certainly known. By
what means has your wisdom revealed such a knowledge in the darkness of such an ignorance? You have
named to us the elements of our present life, and you
have told us, not how they will be transformed—for
that we should not understand—but how they will be
more perfectly reconciled and combined together.
When the magnet unites a filing of iron to itself, it
unites all the filings to that, and to one another. So
you, drawing and reconciling us to yourself, will reconcile us with one another, with ourselves and the
world of your creation." [3]

God has the Last Word over Creation

The New Testament succeeded in holding together
what we have allowed to drift apart—the ultimate destiny of the individual human soul and the ultimate
destiny of the whole created order. But in its doctrine
of the end of things—'eschatology' to use the trade-term
—the New Testament had a simple formula of the
imminent end of the world which few can now believe
in the form in which the first generation of Christians
understood it. A few biblical literalists try to recapture
what they believe the New Testament Christians to have
believed. But in so far as they are trying to recapture
a vanished situation, they are bound to miss its essence.
For it was the essence of the primitive belief that 'the
End' was *literally* near. The fact that it did not happen
alters the whole picture. You can rationalise (or re-
mythologise) the belief by saying that what it really
means is that all points in time are equi-distant from
eternity. If you can give that statement any meaning, it
is true. But it is not the same as believing that the whole

[3] A. M. Farrer, *Lord, I Believe* (S.P.C.K., 1962).

created order will come to an end in the near future—
not by some folly of man, nuclear or contaminating or
genetic; but by the specific will and intervention of an
Almighty Father.

Modern man has another expectation. We know more
about the fantastic length of the evolutionary process
and the range of inter-stellar space. We know that, if
we do not destroy it, life in this infinitesimally small
corner of space can expect to continue for very long
periods of life-bearing conditions. We also know that,
for the first time in that very long story, man has the
capacity totally to destroy life on this planet. Can we
face that possibility and still remain sane? "Human kind
can not bear very much reality." But the scale of
catastrophe has no essential connection with its in-
tensity, and one of the marks of biblical faith is to be
able to face intense catastrophe without despair. It is
one of the characteristics of the God whom the Bible
declares that he is faithful to his promise in spite of the
utmost folly or rebellion on the part of man.

One of the deepest needs of modern man is to discover a *content* to hope which satisfies all the needs of
the spirit which were met by the biblical eschatology.
All theology is in part conditioned by the needs and
character of the age in which it is formulated, so that it
is no denial of the validity of this search to say that it
must be answered in terms which the modern mind finds
real. Many moving formulations are being made [4] but
nowhere, I believe, more movingly and persuasively
than in a writer to whom I have already referred, Pierre
Teilhard de Chardin. Here, from the epilogue of *Le*

[4] Among German writers, notably Jurgen Moltmann, *Theology
of Hope*, translated by J. W. Leitch (S.C.M. Press, 1967).

Milieu Divin is one expression of the way he hears God
have the last word over creation.

"One day, the Gospel tells us, the tension gradually
accumulating between humanity and God will touch
the limits prescribed by the possibilities of the world.
And then will come the end. Then the presence of
Christ, which has been silently accruing in things,
will suddenly be revealed—like a flash of light from
pole to pole. Breaking through all the barriers within
which the veil of matter and the water-tightness of
souls have seemingly kept it confined, it will invade
the face of the earth. And, under the finally-liberated
action of the true affinities of being, the spiritual
atoms of the world will be borne along by a force
generated by the powers of cohesion proper to the
universe itself, and will occupy, whether within Christ
or without Christ (but always under the influence of
Christ), the place of happiness or pain designated for
them by the living structure of the Pleroma.

"Like lightning, like a conflagration, like a flood,
the attraction exerted by the Son of Man will lay hold
of all the whirling elements in the universe so as to
reunite them or subject them to His body.

"Such will be the consummation of the divine
milieu.

"As the Gospel warns us, it would be vain to specu-
late as to the hour and the modalities of this for-
midable event. But we have to *expect* it.

"Expectation—anxious, collective, and operative
expectation of an end of the world, that is to say of
an issue for the world—this is perhaps the supreme
Christian function and the most distinctive characteristic of our religion.

"We have gone deeply into these new perspectives: the progress of the universe, and in particular of the human universe, does not take place in competition with God, nor does it squander energies that we rightly owe to Him. The greater man becomes, the more humanity becomes united ... the more beautiful creation will be, the more perfect adoration will become, and the more Christ will find, for mystical extensions, a body worthy of resurrection. The world can no more have two summits than a circumference can have two centres. The star for which the world is waiting, without yet being able to give it a name, or rightly appreciate its true transcendence, or even recognise the most spiritual and divine of its rays, is, necessarily, Christ Himself, in whom we hope." [5]

[5] Op cit., pp. 147, 148, 151.

Index

Index